TAO TE
CHING

PENGUIN CLASSICS DELUXE EDITION

老子道德經

廖新田

TAO TE CHING

(DAODEJING)

THE TAO AND THE POWER

LAO-TZU

(Laozi)

Translated with an Introduction and Commentary by

JOHN MINFORD

PENGUIN BOOKS

PENGUIN BOOKS

An imprint of Penguin Random House LLC
penguinrandomhouse.com

First published in the United States of America by Viking,
an imprint of Penguin Random House LLC, 2018
Published in Penguin Books 2019

Calligraphy by Liao Hsin-tien
Image on page 311 from *Xingming shuangxiu wanshen
guizhi*, first published in 1615.

ISBN 9780143133803 (paperback)

THE LIBRARY OF CONGRESS HAS CATALOGED THE HARDCOVER EDITION AS FOLLOWS:
Names: Laozi, author. | Minford, John, translator, editor.
Title: Tao te ching (Daodejing) : The tao and the power / Lao-tzu (Laozi) ;
translated with an introduction and commentary by John Minford.
Other titles: Dao de jing. English
Description: New York : Viking, [2018] | Includes bibliographical references and index. |
Identifiers: LCCN 2018030175 (print) | LCCN 2018038136 (ebook) | ISBN 9780525560319 (ebook) |
ISBN 9780670024988 (hardcover)
Subjects: | BISAC: Body, Mind & Spirit / Spiritualism. | Philosophy / Taoist. |
Religion / Taoism (see also Philosophy / Taoist).
Classification: LCC BL1900.L26 (ebook) | LCC BL1900.L26 E5 2018 (print) |
DDC 299.5/1482—dc23
LC record available at https://lccn.loc.gov/2018030175

Printed in the United States of America
6th Printing

Set in Minion Pro
Designed by Cassandra Garruzzo

CONTENTS

INTRODUCTION

This little book is the founding text of China's ancient and enduring religious philosophy, known in the West as Taoism. Taoism, with its history of two and a half millennia, is usually depicted in stark contrast with China's other main traditional philosophy, the secular ideology known in the West as Confucianism, whose founding text is another equally short early work, *The Analects of Confucius (Lunyu)*.[1] Broadly speaking, we may say that Confucianism as it evolved in subsequent centuries emphasized the need for order, respectful harmony within family and society, coded ritual, precise terminology, clearly delineated duty, and structured hierarchy in daily life. Taoism, on the other hand, emphasized inner freedom, meditation, and the Self-Cultivation of the individual, surrender to the spontaneous rhythms of nature, primordial intuition, and exploration of the mysteries of the human condition and the wonders of the cosmos, listening to the silent music of the Tao.

The Tao and the Power (Daodejing) is attributed to a shadowy figure known as Lao-tzu (the Old Master),[2] while the book known as *The Analects* contains the enigmatic and often delightfully eccentric sayings, as recorded by his circle of disciples, of a well-documented historical personality, the peripatetic teacher Confucius (Kongzi, 551–479 BC).[3] Confucius lived toward the very end of what is known as the Spring and Autumn period (771–ca. 475 BC), during which the Zhou dynastic royal house, forced to move its capital eastwards in 771 by the incursions of the Quanrong or "Dog" barbarians, began to suffer the erosion of its central authority while several lesser states contended for power. The more stable earlier half of the dynasty (the Western Zhou, ca. 1046–771 BC) had previously seen the gradual emergence of a written culture and the appearance of such formative pre-philosophical compendia as the oracular *Book of Change* (the *I Ching*), with its sixty-four Hexagrams and its wide-ranging and thought-provoking prognostications, and the *Book of Songs*, with its enchanting repertoire of early folksong and dynastic hymns.[4] These collections were eventually to be enshrined as Classics in the official Confucian canon, often undergoing tortuous ideological distortions in the process. Meanwhile in the southern state of Chu, shamanistic poets had begun to sing with a very different and less restrained voice, one that venerated magic, nature, and the supernatural, in which the individual yearned for erotic and mystical union with the divine.⁵ This was the earliest outpouring of Chinese expressive lyricism. Taoism had much in common with this softer and more exotic southern world, and many have claimed that it had its origins there, whereas Confucian thought grew out of the harsher climes of the central plain and the north, especially the rocky eastern area of the states of Qi and Lu (homeland of Confucius), which now form the Province of Shandong.

TWO MASTERS: LAO-TZU AND CONFUCIUS

Legend has it that the two Masters met more than once, Lao-tzu being somewhat senior to Confucius. In a probably apocryphal chapter of the later *The Book of Taoist Master Zhuang*, their encounters are described with a mischievously mocking Taoist sense of humor.

> Confucius had reached the age of fifty-one and still had not "heard the Tao." Finally he went south to Pei and called on Lao-tzu.
>
> "Ah, here you are!" said Lao-tzu. "I've heard of you as a worthy man from the north. Have you attained the Tao?"
>
> "Not yet," replied Confucius.
>
> "How have you sought it?"
>
> "I sought it through rules and regulations. Five years went by and I could not attain it."
>
> "How else did you seek it?" asked Lao-tzu.
>
> "I sought it in the Yin and the Yang. Twelve years went by and still I could not attain it."
>
> "Of course not!" replied Lao-tzu. "The Tao cannot be sought in this manner . . . The *perfecti* of olden times wandered freely in the wilds, they found nourishment in the fields of Simplicity, they took their stand in the garden of No-Giving. They abode in Non-Action, and found easy nourishment. Their wanderings brought them to the True Tao. This was their Wealth . . ."
>
> Confucius called on Lao-tzu again and this time asked him about the Virtues of Benevolence and Righteousness.
>
> Lao-tzu replied:
>
> "When chaff from the winnowing fan blinds the eyes, then Heaven, Earth, and the Four Directions all appear to be out of place.

The sting of a mosquito or of a horsefly can keep a man awake all night. Similarly, these so-called Virtues of yours do nothing but muddle the mind and cause confusion. Let the world cleave instead to Simplicity and the Uncarved Block. Let it move freely with the wind, and abide in Inner Power. Don't go around huffing and puffing, beating a big drum as if to chase an errant child! The snow goose needs no daily bath to stay white. The crow needs no daily ink to stay black . . ."

When Confucius returned from this visit to Lao-tzu, he was silent for three days. His disciples questioned him, saying:

"When you met Lao-tzu, what advice did you give him?"

"Finally," replied Confucius, "I have set eyes on a Dragon! A Dragon that coils to show off the extent of its body, that sprawls to display the patterns on its scales. A Dragon that rides on the Breath of the Clouds, and feeds on the purest Yin and Yang. My mouth simply fell open in amazement. How could I possibly offer such a Dragon advice?"[6]

Sima Qian (ca. 145–86 BC), the Grand Historian, recorded a similar encounter, in his biographical sketch of Lao-tzu.

Lao-tzu was from Quren Village in the southern state of Chu. His name was Li Dan, and he was the Zhou Official Archivist. Confucius went to Zhou to ask him about the Rites. Lao-tzu said to him:

"You speak of men who have long decayed together with their bones. Nothing but their words has survived. When a Gentleman is in tune with the times, he rides a carriage; when he is out of tune, he makes his way disheveled as he is. I have heard that just as the best merchant keeps his stores hidden so that he appears to possess nothing, so the True Gentleman conceals his abundant Inner Power beneath an appearance of foolishness. Rid yourself of Pride and Desire, put aside your fancy manner and your lustful ways. They will bring you nothing but harm. That is all I have to say."

After he had taken his leave of Lao-tzu, Confucius said to his disciples: "Birds fly; fishes swim; animals run. These things I know. Whatsoever runs can be trapped; whatsoever swims can be caught in a net; whatsoever flies can be brought down with an arrow. But a Dragon riding the clouds into the Heavens—that is quite beyond my comprehension! Today I have seen Lao-tzu. He is like a Dragon!"

Lao-tzu cultivated the Tao and the Inner Power. He advocated the hermit's life, a life lived in obscurity. He lived in Zhou for a long time, but when he saw that the Zhou dynasty was in a state of decline, he departed. When he reached the Pass, the Keeper of the Pass Yin Xi said to him: "You sir are about to retire into seclusion, I beseech you to write a book for me!" So Lao-tzu wrote a book in two parts, treating of the Tao and the Power, in a little over five thousand words. And then he went on his way . . . No one was able to tell who he really was, no one knew where he went to in the end . . . He was a recluse.[7]

The two accounts differ in many ways, but they have in common the vision of Lao-tzu as that transcendent, most auspicious and most powerful creature, a Dragon. He is portrayed as someone with a truly remarkable charisma, someone whose *mana* made a deep and lasting impression, a Great Man, a genuine Immortal riding the clouds. Truly, in the words of the *I Ching*:

> The Dragon
> Flies in Heaven.
> *Draco Volans in coelo.*
> It profits
> To see a Great Man.

The Great Man is the Dragon. The Yang which has been slowly accumulating is suddenly transformed, it attains perfect freedom. The soaring flight is free, effortless, and unhampered. The Sage simply takes off, following the Tao as naturally and instinctively as if it were an Edict of Heaven.[8]

THE HUNDRED SCHOOLS

In both of these little books, *The Analects* of Confucius and Lao-tzu's *The Tao and the Power*, the Chinese literary language reached a new level of coherence and expressive power; it acquired the potential to articulate more complex and subtle ideas. They were most probably both compiled at the beginning of the period of still further intensified turmoil and civil war known as the Warring States (ca. 475–221 BC), which witnessed the final disintegration of the Zhou dynasty and the ultimate unification of China under the harsh totalitarian rule of the northwestern state of Qin. These chaotic centuries saw the rise of many contending schools of thought across China, the so-called Hundred Schools, all of whom were "Disputers of the Tao," claiming to possess a recipe, a Way, or Tao, for both the individual and the ruler, for living and statecraft.[9] One such school, known as the Legalists or the School of Law (*fajia*), advocated a drastic totalitarian solution to government, and this was the way of thinking followed by the Ruler of Qin, infamous builder of the Great Wall and (according to some) burner of the books.[10] A short work from this same period, *The Art of War* (*Sunzi bingfa*), is attributed to another shadowy figure, a strategist known as Master Sun (Sunzi, more familiar in its old spelling, Sun-tzu). It is a startlingly Machiavellian treatise in praise of cunning and subterfuge, which cleverly exploits some of the softer and more attractive kungfu-like maxims of early Taoism.

> Military dispositions take form like water: water shuns the high and hastens to the low. War shuns the strong and attacks the weak. Water shapes its current from the lie of the land. The warrior shapes his victory from the dynamic of the enemy.[11]

TAOISM AND CONFUCIANISM IN HISTORY

The thinking of Confucius was further developed by two later Confucian figures, Mencius (Mengzi, or Meng-tzu, ca. 372–289 BC) and Master Xun (Xunzi, or Hsün-tzu, ca. 310–235 BC), whose books contain more sustained philosophical argumentation than is to be found in *The Analects*. In a similar way, the Taoist master-raconteur Master Zhuang (Zhuangzi, or Chuang-tzu, fourth century BC) and his followers brilliantly elaborated the leading ideas of *The Tao and the Power*. Other Taoist compendia followed (such as *The Book of the Huainan Master*, and the later *Book of Master Lie*).[12] Under the Han dynasty (206 BC–AD 220), Confucianism eclipsed Taoism to become established as the dominant state ideology of China, remaining so for over two thousand years, with the occasional hiatus. Chinese public life was thenceforth rooted in the precepts of Confucianism, and every educated individual had to pass a series of grueling examinations on the Confucian canon. But Taoism continued to flourish nonetheless, with monasteries and hermitages on every mountain, and proliferating lineages of Masters and Schools teaching a variety of meditational practices, guiding the seeker toward the Tao. It was in effect the all-pervading undercurrent of Chinese culture, later fusing with other ways of thinking, helping to give birth to the school of Buddhism known as Chan (*Zen* in Japanese) and deeply influencing the Neo-Confucian revival of the Song dynasty (960–1279).

ART AND LITERATURE

Taoism also permeated the Chinese literary and artistic worlds. The painter Zong Bing (375–443) captured the Taoist ideal of artistic inspiration:

> The Sage embraces the Tao and responds harmoniously to things . . . And so I dwell in leisure and nourish my Breath-Energy. I drain my wine-cup, pluck the *qin*, I unroll painted scrolls and gaze at landscapes in silence. Though seated, I travel beyond the four borders of the land, never leaving the realm of nature, and responding in my solitude to the call of the wilderness. Cliffs and peaks rise before me to soaring heights, and dense groves of trees extend amid clouds into the furthest distance . . . Every delight in the universe comes together in Spirit and Thought. What else do I have need of? I give full and free rein to Spirit. That is all. What could be more important than this?[13]

In his "Twenty-Four Modes of Poetry," Sikong Tu (837–908), like so many writers in all periods of Chinese history, traced the source of all literary creation to the Tao:

> *The Tao of Nature*
> Stoop down and there it is;
> Seek it neither right nor left.
> All roads lead thither—
> One touch and spring is present.
> It is like coming upon flowers in bloom,
> Like gazing at the advent of the year . . .
> I am like a hermit on a lonely hill . . .
> My words are scant and beyond emotion,
> In the distant Harmony of Heaven . . .
>
> *Free*
> Through the Tao I return to Breath-Energy,
> Free and unrestrained,
> Flowing like the wind of Heaven,

Lofty as mountains and seas,
Sun, moon, and stars before me . . .[14]

Music too was Union with the Tao, especially the delicate music played on the seven-stringed *qin*.

> If you wish to play the *qin*, you must light incense, and sit in silent meditation. Empty the mind of outward thoughts. Poise Breath and Blood in Perfect Harmony. Your soul may now commune with Spirit, and enter into that mysterious Union with the Tao.[15]

Over the centuries, many a Chinese scholar-official would return from his government *yamen* or official workplace to the seclusion of his private studio or *zhai*, where he would quietly practice a sort of "weekend Taoism," writing occasional verse, indulging his love of painting and calligraphy, playing a game of Go, plucking the strings of his *qin*, and enjoying the other pastimes of the leisured man of letters, all of which had as their goal the fusion of the individual with the Tao of the cosmos. He did not feel this to be incompatible with his sterner weekday Confucian public persona. Any complete study of traditional China, and indeed of contemporary China, any understanding of the complex light and shade of Chinese society and culture, requires a knowledge of both these strands: the Confucian and the Taoist.

ORIGINS OF THE CHINESE CLASSIC

What of the original Chinese text of *The Tao and the Power* itself? Its origins and authorship are (appropriately enough) shrouded in the mists of legend and mystery. It has always been associated with the name of Lao-tzu. But as we have already seen, China's great historian Sima Qian concludes that "no one was able to tell who Lao-tzu really was, no one knew where he went to in the end . . . He was a recluse."[16] He was in other words a Chinese hermit, of the kind one sees in innumerable later Chinese landscapes, a tiny figure communing with Nature, dwarfed by mighty mountains and waterfalls. Isabelle Robinet has given this brief modern account of the book (brief because there are indeed so few reliable facts):

> The work is ascribed to Lao-tzu, who allegedly gave it to a border guard named Yin Xi as he left the Middle Kingdom to go to the west. Scholars have long debated its authorship and date. Some think that

it is not the work of a single author, some maintain that most of it originated as oral tradition during the Warring States period (475–221 BC).[17]

Arthur Waley (1889–1966) comments in a similar vein that parts of the work seem to stem from early Taoist hymns, from what he calls the "general stock of early Taoist rhymed teaching." D. C. Lau, writing in 1963, argued that the work was an "anthology compiled by more than one hand."[18] I tend toward this view. We now know for sure (from irrefutable archaeological evidence) that a text of the Classic existed at least as early as the late fourth century BC. (The slightly different "received text" or vulgate, with its division into eighty-one chapters, dates from the Han dynasty, several centuries later.) In 1973 and 1993, early copies were found in two separate excavated tombs. Two were written on silk and are almost complete. They are datable to before 168 BC, and were excavated in 1973 at Mawangdui in the suburbs of Changsha, capital city of the modern Province of Hunan, from the tomb of a marquis of the southern state of Chu. Another more fragmentary copy, written on bamboo slips, was excavated in 1993 at the village of Guodian in southern Hubei Province, near the site of the ancient capital of Chu. It is datable to just before 300 BC, and was found in the tomb of a lesser dignitary, probably a Royal Tutor.[19] Since my own understanding (and hence translation) of the book is primarily based on the later commentaries of Heshang Gong (the River Master) and Magister Liu Yiming, the text I follow is in the main theirs, the later received text, although very occasionally I have made reference to variations found in the silk or bamboo texts.

A WORDLESS TEACHING

Beautiful Words are not to be Trusted. Many Words are soon spent. To be sparing with Words is the Tao of Nature. The Taoist practices a Wordless Teaching.[20]

The Tao and the Power proclaims at the very outset the inadequacy of Words to communicate the Mystery of the Tao, to convey the deeper Knowledge that is No-Knowledge.

The Tao that can be Told is not the True Tao. Who Knows does not speak; Who speaks does not Know. Many Words Harm the Person. If the Mouth keeps opening, if the Tongue keeps wagging, Misfortune will surely follow.[21]

And yet its Five Thousand Words boldly attempt to Tell the Untellable. This dilemma has haunted would-be Tellers (and Translators, or Re-Tellers) of the Tao down the ages, to the present day. A recently published glossary entry for the Word *Tao* reads like a brilliant (and somewhat inebriated, Humpty Dumpty–like) parody of this dilemma.

> To say that the Tao is the origin, totality, and animating impulse of all that is, ever was, and ever shall be is inadequate, for this would exclude what is not, never was, and never shall be . . . It is ultimately Ineffable . . .[22]

Despite the sheer scale and Ineffability of its subject, *The Tao and the Power* has been read by millions of Chinese readers down the years, has provided them with abundant spiritual nourishment, and is still avidly read today. It is still felt to be relevant. "At a time when officials of particular nations on earth are vying to vaunt the ability of their leadership, or the merit of their incomparable power," wrote the great scholar Anthony C. Yu in 2003, "even in the looming shadow of catastrophic conflict, the wisdom of *The Tao and the Power* seems ever more compelling and urgent."[23] It is one of the most powerful attempts to find Words for a Wordless Truth. It has had a profound and lasting influence on Chinese ways of thinking; it has molded the Chinese Heart-and-Mind. That's why it has survived.

THE TAO

The single word *Tao* (or *Dao* in its modern spelling), from which the term *Taoism* is derived, is shared by many Chinese schools of thought. One of its literal meanings is "way" or "road." In later centuries, in common parlance, Tao came to mean little more than what we would call the Art, or Fundamental Principle: the Tao of Music, the Tao of Tea, the Tao of Painting or Calligraphy or Poetry, etc. Another old and fundamental meaning of the word is to "tell" or "say," to verbalize, to find Words for ideas, somewhat akin to the *logos* of early Western philosophy. Hence the word play of the book's opening line: the Tao that can be verbalized or *Tao*-ed is not the True Tao. Joseph Needham gave his own inimitable explanation of the word:

> Tao is the Order of Nature, which brought all things into existence and governs their every action, not so much by force as by a kind of natural curvature in space and time. It reminds us of the *logos* of Heraclitus.[24]

Richard Wilhelm, the German sinologist, rhapsodized (very much in the style of the Book and its Commentators):

> Tao is earlier than Heaven and Earth. One cannot tell whence it comes . . . It rests upon itself, it is immutable, rapt in eternal, cyclical movement. It is the beginning of Heaven and Earth, in other words, of temporal and spatial existence.[25]

THE TAOIST

The Tao itself cannot easily be Told. But can we at least say a bit about what a Taoist, a Seeker of the Tao, is like, what a Taoist thinks and does, how a Taoist lives? The trouble is, as the Book itself reminds us, such people can only be seen with great difficulty. They don't identify themselves in public, they don't shine, they don't show off their Tao, their Inner Power. They are essentially incognito. One can at best form a vague impression of them.

> Of Old Taoists were Subtle and Marvelous, Darkly Connected, Deep beyond all Knowing. Since they could never be Known, let us tell how they seemed: Hesitant, as though crossing a stream in winter . . . Melting, like Ice at first Thaw; Simple, like a Block of Uncarved Wood; Broad as a Valley; Murky as Mud.[26]

The Taoist often appears drab and undistinguished.

> I alone am forlorn and quiet, I am listless, with no place to go, a poor rustic with no Home, a derelict.

The Taoists keep their Light hidden.

> As the old saying goes: The Light of the Tao seems Dark. The Taoist glows with a Contained Light, the Dark Light of Spirit.[27]

The Taoist's Knowledge is the Inner Knowledge of the Initiate, of the Adept. With it the Taoist Understands everything.

> Without setting foot outside the door, the Taoist Knows All-under-Heaven. The Taoist Understands with the Knowledge of Spirit,

has no need to set foot outside, has no need to look through the window. The Taoist sees with the Vision of Spirit, Darkly One with the Tao of Heaven-and-Nature. The Taoist Understands everything with the Inner Eye, sees the Tao everywhere, in everything.[28]

THE POWER

So the Taoist is hard to spot and describe, and the Tao itself is Untellable and therefore Untranslatable. (The word itself is indeed best "retold"—i.e., "transliterated"—as *Tao*.) But what can be said of the Power of the Tao, the second word, *Te* (modern *De*), of the Book's title, *The Tao and the Power*, or *Tao Te Ching* (modern *Daodejing*—a title it acquired only after many centuries)? In Waley's words, it is a "latent" power, an inherent "virtue" (in the old sense). It is the Inner Power or *mana* attained by the Taoist Adept through Self-Cultivation, "by virtue" of which, by emanating which, the Taoist can mysteriously influence everyone and everything in the Universe. The Dutch scholar Jan Duyvendak (1889–1954) called it a "magical life-force, the influence radiating from one link to the next in the interminable chain" of Cosmic Resonance and Correspondence which is the Tao. The Taoist tunes into this life-force, which operates or emanates without conscious effort. It is also described variously as the Power of the Infant, the Power of Not-Contending, the Power of Non-Action. Every Taoist reader of this little text, every Seeker of the Tao, accumulates a reservoir of this Energy and Power, this gentle Source of Strength. It is a Power that makes itself felt in everyday life, and although the teaching of the Classic is often mystical and enigmatic, its applications are deeply practical and unpretentious. The Taoist mystic or *perfectus* has a wonderful sense of humor, a twinkle in his eye. He knows, after all, that governing a large state is like cooking a small fish.

COMMENTARIES, THE LINEAGE OF THE LIGHT

Ever since the text of *The Tao and the Power* first began circulating, right up to the present day, many hundreds of Chinese Commentators have tried their hand at making its deliberately misty "meaning" clearer, at "adumbrating" the Tao.[29] One of these was the eighteenth-century practicing Taoist monk Liu Yiming, whom I personally find most compelling. Here is a brief extract from his Commentary:

The Five Thousand Words of *The Tao and the Power* give us in-klings of the Origin, of the Mother, they reveal the Inner Working of the Spiritual Mysteries of the Tao. The Root of the Tao lies in Em-bracing the One, in Non-Action. The Tao is Soft and Gentle, it does Not Contend. Through Emptiness and lasting Calm, through a Re-turn to the Root, a Return to Simplicity and Purity, to True Life-Destiny, the Taoist reaps the full Benefits of Life. Taoist Self-Cultivation enables All-Under-Heaven to be well Ordered, to be at Peace. For every person, from the Son of Heaven to the humblest commoner, this Truth Prevails: that to bring Order to Others one must first Order Self, that Self-Cultivation is the Root of all.[30] [. . .] Hold Fast, Forget Words, Nurture Breath-Energy, be at Peace with Nature, with the So-of-Itself, be Calm and Still.[31]

This and many other Commentaries have a strange language of their own, they transmit a powerful message, they are a link in what the Classic itself calls the Lineage of the Light. It is my sincere hope that as the reader pro-gresses through my translation of the text and its Commentaries, these at-first-sight-impenetrable Taoist improvisations around a Wordless Teaching will gradually acquire a Resonance and become more meaningful.

TWO CHOSEN COMMENTARIES

To Know the Spirit of the Valley, seek guidance from a True Teacher. Without such a Teacher, all is vain speculation, and the Spirit will remain elusive.[32]

Two Chinese Commentators, separated by roughly two millennia, have served as my principal Teachers and Guides for this new version. They were both concerned to apply the teachings of Lao-tzu to the Taoist Practice of Self-Cultivation. The first, Heshang Gong, the River Master, is a figure every bit as legendary as Lao-tzu himself. The legend is worth giving.

The River Master is said to have lived during the reign of fifth Emperor Wen (203–157 BC) of the Western Han dynasty. The Em-peror greatly venerated Lao-tzu's *The Tao and the Power*. He heard tell of a Hermit called the River Master, and sent emissaries to sum-mon him for clarification of certain obscurities in the scripture. The

River Master insisted on seeing the sovereign in person at his hermitage, and eventually Emperor Wen sought him out and found him
seated in a humble hut by the banks of the Yellow River. There he
haughtily demanded instruction. The Master by way of response at
first remained seated motionless where he was, then clapped his
hands together, and rose a hundred or so feet into the air. He remained there floating in mid-air, and eventually addressed a string
of mysterious words to the Emperor. The Emperor fell to his knees,
this time begging for enlightenment. The Master, impressed at last
by the Emperor's humility and sincerity, presented him with his
Commentary on *The Tao and the Power* written on two silken scrolls.
"Go home and read this carefully," he said, "and you will be able to
put all doubt behind you. It is many hundreds of years since I first
wrote this Commentary, and you are only the fourth person ever to
read it—do not divulge a word to another living soul." With these
words the Master vanished, and a thick mist descended, shrouding
everything in darkness. The Emperor knew that he had encountered
a True Immortal, a Perfectus of the Tao, and gave orders for a terrace
to be constructed in the hills to the west of the River, in the hope of
sighting him once more. He never did see him again however, but
treasured the Master's Commentary for the rest of his days.[33]

The second Commentator I have followed is Liu Yiming (1734–1821), whom
I have already quoted above. He will be familiar to readers of my translation
of the *I Ching*, in which I gave lengthy extracts from his *I Ching* Commentary.
Magister Liu, as I call him, was a High Master of the Quanzhen (Complete
Reality) Taoist sect, and was known by various other Taoist names, including
Master of Primordial Enlightenment (*wuyuanzi*) and Vagabond of Simple
Silk and the Uncarved Block (*supu sanren*). He also wrote, among many other
things, a Commentary on the Ming dynasty novel *Journey to the West*. He
was a remarkable individual, who brought to his reading of both the *I Ching*
and *The Tao and the Power* insights from his own life in the Tao. During his
late teens, he suffered a nearly fatal illness, and was restored to health by a
Taoist monk. This changed his life. He set off wandering around remote areas
of China, "seeking the Tao," until at the age of twenty-two, in the northwest,
he encountered a Taoist Hermit known as the Old Man of the Valley of the
Sacred Shrine, who initiated him into the discipline of *neidan*, or Inner Alchemy. This branch of Taoist Practice is no mystical mumbo jumbo, but a
carefully thought-out and long-established method of Self-Cultivation or

Self-Development, "a technique of enlightenment, a method of controlling both the world and oneself, a process of existential and intellectual integration."[34] In many ways, it is startlingly modern. After many further years of Self-Cultivation of this sort and more wandering around in China's remoter regions, encountering another Teacher, doing all sorts of odd jobs, Liu finally settled in his own hermitage in the mountains (he called it his Den of Freedom, *zizai wo*), offering Taoist teachings and macrobiotic medical advice to all comers. He wrote large quantities of Taoist-inspired verse, which I find extremely reminiscent of the zany "Won-Done Song" chanted by the Taoist monk in the first chapter of the novel *The Story of the Stone* (after all, Liu was a near contemporary of that novel's main author, Cao Xueqin).

> *Men all know that salvation should be won,*
> *But with ambition won't have done.*
> *Where are the famous ones of days gone by?*
> *In grassy graves they lie now, every one.*[35]

It is so easy to imagine Liu as one of the disheveled monks with whom that novel's hero Jia Bao-yu wanders off into the snow in the very last chapter, chanting:

> *Who will explore*
> *The supremely Ineffable*
> *Vastly Mysterious*
> *Wilderness*
> *To which I Return?*[36]

Magister Liu wrote two Commentaries on *The Tao and the Power*, a long and rather involved one (*Daodejing huiyi*) and a much shorter one for the benefit of readers who found the long one too complex (*Daodejing yaoyi*). I have consulted both, translating them first in their entirety, and then running them freely into one.

I have substantially simplified and shortened both of these Commentaries, trying to avoid unnecessary and unhelpful repetition (of which there is a great deal) and steering clear of arcane alchemical interpretations, which would have made this a very different book.[37] What I present is essentially my personal condensation of their Taoistic ramblings, with a view to casting light on the spiritual message of the original text, making it meaningful and relevant today.

RHYME

Three quarters of the Chinese text of *The Tao and the Power*, as the Swedish philologist Bernhard Karlgren has shown, rhymes, when read according to the reconstructed phonetic values of Ancient Chinese. This gives it an underlying resonance, making it memorable and chantable. Take for example Chapter 6, the Valley Spirit. In modern Mandarin the rhyme is partly detectable, but the older pronunciation (approximate values in square brackets) makes the rhyme even more obvious:

> *Gu shen bu si [si]*
> *Shi wei xuan pin. [bj'i]*
> *Xuan pin zhi men, [muen]*
> *Shi wei tian di gen. [ken]*
> *Mian mian ruo cun [dz'uen]*
> *Yong zhi bu qin. [gien]*[38]

I have not attempted a rhyming translation. But I have tried to keep my version as terse as possible, choosing a simple vocabulary, with an inevitable admixture of Taoist "terms for the initiate," which I have usually capitalized. I have also broken the main text into short centered lines, to indicate something of the poetic and aphoristic quality of the Chinese original. This quality is both daunting and inspiring for the translator. It is after all the poetic magic and music that brings us closer to the Ineffable Inner Core of meaning. As Waley memorably wrote, it "flings across intervening space a mere filament such as no sober foot would dare to tread . . . Its Inner Power so intoxicates us that, endowed with the recklessness of drunken men, we dance across the chasm, hardly aware how we reached the other side."[39] It would require a far greater gift than mine to recreate the ancient poetic Power of these Chinese lines, to capture their "dearest freshness deep down things," "the achieve of, the mastery of the thing."[40]

IMAGES AND THEMES

The Tao and the Power employs powerful Symbols and Images to point to the Ineffable, and weaves around its central Wordless Teaching a mesmerizing cycle of Taoist Themes. The Themes are makeshift Names ("the Names that can be Named are not True Names") for aspects of Taoist Teaching.

They form an interlocking code for stages in the spiritual process, for the "existential and intellectual integration" of Self-Cultivation. All of these Images and Themes are connected; they are part of an organic system of ideas. To Understand One is to Understand All. For example, it is hard to Understand the significance of Water as a principal Image and Symbol of the Tao without Understanding the related Themes of Non-Action and Not-Contending, and vice versa. The book proceeds in an intuitive, poetic, non-logical, zigzag, often repetitive, and sometimes incoherent fashion. To help readers new to this whole Taoist way of thinking, and to illustrate certain of the book's key Images and Themes, I have selected and grouped together certain striking terms from both the original text and the Commentaries and appended them at the end of my translation, in the section I have called my "Florilegium of the Tao."

TAOISM TODAY

In 1968, the Beatles recorded George Harrison's classic song "The Inner Light," which they later released as the B-side of "Lady Madonna." Harrison's lyrics are a simple variation on Chapter 47 of *The Tao and the Power*. Similarly, the opening lines of his 1970 song "All Things Must Pass" also derive from the Taoist Classic. They were inspired by a reading of the LSD guru Timothy Leary's 1966 *Psychedelic Prayers after the Tao Te Ching*, and go back ultimately to Chapter 23 of *The Tao and the Power*:

> A whirlwind doesn't last all morning,
> A cloudburst doesn't last all day.

In other words, the Tao is still alive and well. It is constantly being recast in a host of different shapes, and has continued to fascinate the Western mind, working its timeless magic on the likes of psychotherapist Carl Jung, novelist Hermann Hesse, on Alan Watts, Gary Snyder, and the Beat Generation, and on fantasy writer Ursula K. Le Guin. It has turned up in some quite unlikely places—such as Benjamin Hoff's *The Tao of Pooh*.[41]

As the eminent American sinologist Arthur W. Hummel (1884–1975) wrote in 1962, the scripture, which first came into being "in the morning of the human race," still "bears the freshness of the morning upon it."[42] Or as Joseph Needham noted, Taoism is "a program for our time as well as theirs."[43]

PREVIOUS TRANSLATIONS

This new version of mine is the latest in a very long line of translations into Western languages. The very earliest translation, an unpublished Latin manuscript version by a Jesuit, was presented as a gift to the Royal Society in London in 1788. In the early stages of this long lineage, there was an overwhelming tendency to regard all Chinese scriptures as divinely inspired. They were the words of a Christian God speaking Chinese, hence the misguided but strongly held eighteenth-century Jesuit Figurist belief that the *I Ching* was the Lost Book of Enoch . . . In the seventeenth century, two Jesuits, Philippe Couplet (1622–1693) and Louis le Comte (1655–1728), both claimed to recognize in the Taoist Classic references to the Holy Trinity, as in Chapter 42:

> The Tao gave Birth to the One.
> The One gave Birth to the Two.
> The Two gave Birth to the Three.
> The Three gave Birth to the Myriad Things . . .

They interpreted the opening words of Chapter 14 in the same way:

> These three merge into the One,
> They form the Ineffable Whole of the Tao . . .

These hallucinations continued well into the nineteenth century.[44] Jean-Pierre Abel-Rémusat (1788–1832), first professor of sinology at the Collège de France, in his Commentary on Chapter 14, identified three Chinese words as "originally Hebrew."

> Look, and you can never see it—
> It is too *Subtle*.
> Listen, and you can never hear it—
> It is too *Faint*.
> Feel for it, and you can never take hold of it—
> It is too *Elusive*.

The three words, *yi* (which I translate as subtle), *shi* (faint), and *wei* (elusive), were, he declared, "signs for foreign sounds in the Chinese language and appear identical to the Hebrew Tetragrammaton of Jahweh: it is remarkable that the most exact transcription of His celebrated name is to be found in a Chinese book."[45] Now I am only too aware that these three Chinese words are tantalizingly hard to translate, and that my own versions are mere approximations. But they are at least approximations based on the Chinese words themselves. And of one thing I am quite sure: those words have nothing whatsoever to do with Jehovah, just as the *I Ching* had nothing to do with the Lost Book of Enoch! But the habit of Christianizing the Tao died hard. Many years later the German scholar of Old Testament studies Julius Grill (1840–1930) claimed to have discovered no fewer than eighty parallels between the New Testament and *The Tao and the Power*.[46] This may have encouraged him to proclaim the importance of the Classic: "The time of Lao-tzu is now just beginning; he is not a man and a name of the past, but a strength for now and the future. He is more modern than the most modern and more alive than many who are living."[47]

Ex Oriente Lux! By the last decades of the nineteenth century, Western thinkers (such as the Theosophists) had already begun to grow more and more convinced that True Wisdom, a brighter light, a deeper spirituality, would come from the East. Paul Carus (1852–1919), the German scholar who migrated to the United States in 1884, was one of the first to translate the Taoist Classic directly out of the Chinese (in a bilingual format) from the perspective of a universal monism, the philosophical belief that all existence shares a fundamental unity. This trend continued throughout the twentieth century, as well-meaning Seekers of Wisdom and authors of self-help books used the Classic (nearly always in someone else's translation) as a springboard for their own ideas.[48]

WESTERN VOICES OF THE TAO

How have less wayward Western interpreters sought to expound the true (truly Chinese) "business of the Tao," the basic message of *The Tao and the Power*? Arthur Waley, one of the finest translators and interpreters of Chinese poetry and of Chinese mystical thought, ended the Introduction to his 1935 translation with a brief quip from the later Taoist Master Zhuang:

> [According to the Taoists] the soul was looked upon as having become as it were silted up by successive deposits of daily toil and perturbation, and the business of the [Taoist] self-perfecter was to work his way back through these layers till "man as he was meant to

be" was reached ... traveling back through layers of consciousness to the point of Pure Consciousness, to the point where language, created to meet the demands of ordinary, upper consciousness, no longer applies. The Adept who has reached this point has learnt "to get into the bird-cage without setting the birds off singing."[49]

In more recent times, Angus Graham (1919–1991), brilliant philosopher and translator, has captured some of the essential ingredients of the Taoist way of life.

> The Taoist relaxes the body, calms the mind, loosens the grip of categories made habitual by naming, frees the current of thought for more fluid differentiations and assimilations, and instead of pondering choices lets problems solve themselves as inclination spontaneously finds its own direction, which is the Tao. At the deep end is the mystical, at the shallow end Self-Cultivation may serve as a means to relaxation, poise, loosening of habit, creativity, quickening of responsiveness, for the Chinese wrestler or for the Californian businessman using meditative techniques to enhance efficiency.[50]

Graham at the same time acknowledges the difficulties inherent in understanding or translating the Classic and its philosophy:

> *The Tao and the Power*, with its strange and elusive philosophy of life, can only guide us in the Direction of the Tao by way of aphorisms and parable. It is a text with infinite possibilities of divergent interpretation and sheer misunderstanding.[51]

In Waley's words, it is a text full of the "paradoxical twisting-round of other people's maxims," it has "an epigrammatic and pungent quality." And it is literally without time, it is timeless, as is all Chinese classical poetry. Literary Chinese knows no tense. "Every sentence in *The Tao and the Power* refers as much to the past as to the present."

A VERSION FOR *LECTIO SINICA*

The German sinologist Eduard Erkes wrote in 1945 that he wished to help the reader make practical use of the book as a "guide to meditation and to the Taoist life."[52] This has also been my aim. In that sense, I belong to the lineage of Paul Carus, Richard Wilhelm, and Arthur Waley. But it is very much a Chinese lineage too. *The Tao and the Power* has always been used in China "as a sacred text that, like all sacred writings, must be recited in conjunction with meditation and ritual practices for exorcist and healing purposes."[53]

My version, therefore, is not for scholars or intellectuals, but for the purposes of slow meditative reading, a form of *Lectio Sinica*, in the Benedictine monastic tradition of *Lectio Divina*, or Sacred Reading.

> In Sacred Reading the monk or nun would sit with the text of Scripture and begin to read attentively and reflectively until a word or phrase or scene struck the imagination or the heart. At that moment the reader paused, put the text aside, and gave himself or herself to prayer. The prayerful pause might last less than a minute or might be extended for a number of minutes. When attention faltered, the reader would return to the text until another moment of insight or another incentive to love should come along. The rhythm of reading and pausing would continue peacefully, unhurriedly, until the bell announced the next exercise of the monastic day.[54]

Charles Cummings, author of the above, himself a Trappist-Cistercian monk, laments that reading has lost its savor for many in today's culture, having been replaced by a complicated host of devices, by ever more sophisticated (and upgraded) audiovisual media of communication. I wholeheartedly agree. So did Lao-tzu.

> With Cunning Skills, Strange Contraptions and Devices proliferate. So the Taoist says: "I Return to Non-Action."[55]

> The folk Return to the Ancient Tying of Knots.[56]

Magister Liu Yiming expands on this.

> They find Peace in Nature, in the So-of-Itself, in True Resonance and Calm, just as in Ancient Times men kept records with Knotted Ropes.

I first encountered the living tradition of slow meditative reading in December 2016 when I had the great privilege of staying in the Benedictine College of St. Anselm, on the Aventine Hill in Rome.[57] I was then working on the fourth revision of this translation, and the timeless atmosphere of the College's cloisters, the simple calm and orderly rhythm of monastic ritual (including silence at breakfast in the refectory), the resonant Gregorian plainchant sung every evening at Vespers by the monks assembled in the Basilica, merged imperceptibly in my mind with the Chinese words as I worked on the Taoist Classic.

A GUIDE TO EVERYDAY LIVING

So those seeking an intellectual or textual reading of this classic will be disappointed by my translation. More than fifty years ago I first studied this book as an undergraduate at Oxford, with the help of my genial tutor Ian McMorran. I am grateful to him for having encouraged me even then to read it as something more than an academic exercise in textual criticism. I remember vividly traveling with him in his car down Cumnor Hill and noticing the Chinese words *wuwei* (Non-Action) stuck firmly to the dashboard of his car. He also introduced me early on to the work of Waley and Duyvendak, whose insights will be found scattered throughout my Commentary.[58] When I began work on my own version more than five years ago, at the kind suggestion of John Siciliano of Viking in New York, I knew that my priority would still be to convey the book's value as a guide to everyday living. Liu Ts'un-yan (1917–2009), my longtime friend and teacher, was himself a practicing Taoist with an unparalleled knowledge of the history of Taoism. In his later years he always emphasized two things in conversation: (1) that at the heart of Taoist teaching lay the simple perception of what was True (*zhen*) and what was False (*jia*); and (2) that the main value of Taoism was not at all esoteric, it was quite simple, it was to help people lead better, kinder, gentler lives. I have tried to remain faithful to his teaching.[59]

I cannot pretend to know exactly what each phrase of this often baffling Chinese text means. But I have chosen to try and follow my own understanding, guided by the River Master and by Magister Liu, rather than provide the reader with a perplexing array of uncertain readings. That array might have made for an interesting book in its own right (a bit like the fascinating anthology of differing versions of Wang Wei by Eliot Weinberger and Octavio Paz). But it is not what I chose to do.

To the main text I have added my Running Commentary, giving first the thoughts of the River Master and Magister Liu, then a selection of thoughts from others. I decided to end each Chapter with a Chinese poem or a brief extract from a literary essay. Taoist themes permeate Chinese literature, and sometimes a well-written poem seemed to me to shed light on these themes more effectively than any amount of expository or aphoristic prose. The poems I have chosen provide a layman's counterpoint to the sometimes obscure drift of the main text and Commentary. Although sometimes they may seem to be quite unconnected with the preceding Chapter, they take the reader aside into another corner of the Taoist Realm (in which all corners are connected). My own favorites as Exemplars of the Taoist lifestyle have always been those medieval Chinese hippies, the Seven Sages of the Bamboo Grove. Xi Kang, Liu Ling, and Ruan Ji feature prominently here.[60]

THE VALLEY SPIRIT NEVER DIES

It is a basic Taoist conviction that there is a Simple Way to a better and healthier Life, to Long Life in the deeper sense, to a Softer, Gentler, Kinder, more Generous Harmony with Others and with Nature, with the Suchness-of-Self, and of other Beings and Things, with their Essence, their So-of-Itself, with Life-Destiny. The first step on this path or Tao is, in Arthur Waley's words, to be "in Harmony with, not in rebellion against, the fundamental laws of the universe." Attainment of this comes from a changed way of thinking, a bigger, more open Heart-and-Mind. It comes, as Magister Liu would say, from the Transformation of the Human Heart-and-Mind into the Heart-and-Mind of the Tao. Hummel wrote of the book's "mind-stretching quality," of the way it "challenges at every turn, expanding our view of life's possibilities."[61] I hope that this translation of mine, despite its many stumblings and shortcomings, if read in the calm spirit of *Lectio Sinica*, will in some small way convey the powerfully thought-altering quality of this ancient text, and of its Commentators.[62]

My own favorite lines are from the Sixth Chapter:

> The Valley Spirit never Dies.
> The Mystic Feminine,
> The Gate of the Mystic Feminine,
> The Root of Heaven and Earth . . .

Magister Liu comments:

> The Valley Spirit
> Exists for ever,

It is the Mother
Of All Marvels,
Gate of the Mystic Feminine,
Opening and closing
According to season,
It is the Root
Of the Primordial Wonder
Of Heaven and Earth,
Of spontaneous Motion and Stillness,
Of Calm.
Wherever this Spirit is,
There is the Tao.

☵

Done over the years 2010–2017 at Fontmarty, Corbières; Three Dog Hall, Brou-lee; Karori, Wellington; Siu Lek Yuen, Hong Kong; Benedictine College of St. Anselm, Rome; Palazzo Maurogonato, Venice; the French Quarter, Feather-ston, New Zealand.

NOTES

1. See Arthur Waley, tr., *The Analects of Confucius* (London: Allen & Unwin, 1938). See also D. C. Lau's *The Analects* (London: Penguin Classics, 1979); the stimulating translation by Simon Leys (New York: Norton, 1997); and the new Penguin Classics translation by Annping Chin (London: Penguin Classics, 2014).
2. I use the old and familiar spelling, Lao-tzu, as opposed to the modern Laozi.
3. "Confucius" (from the Chinese *kong-fu-zi*) was the latinized name given him by the early Jesuits.
4. For the first see Richard Wilhelm's classic version, translated into English by Cary F. Baynes in two volumes (London: Routledge and Kegan Paul, 1951), and my more recent *I Ching* (New York: Viking, 2016). The best translation of the *Book of Songs* for the general reader remains Arthur Waley's *The Book of Songs* (London: Allen & Unwin, 1937).
5. See *The Songs of the South*, a revised edition translated by David Hawkes (London: Penguin Classics, 1995), especially the sections "Heavenly Questions" and "Nine Songs."
6. Compare Burton Watson, tr., *The Complete Works of Chuang Tzu* (New York: Columbia University Press, 1968), Chapter 14, "The Turning of Heaven," pp. 161ff, on which this translation is based.
7. Extracted from the biography of Lao-tzu in the *Shiji*.
8. The *I Ching, Book of Change*, Hexagram I, Yang in Fifth Place, with commentary based on Wang Fuzhi. John Minford, tr. (New York: Viking, 2014), pp. 21–2.
9. Angus Graham uses the expression "Disputers of the Tao" as the title for his excellent study of early Chinese thought (Chicago: Open Court, 1989).
10. Waley's *Three Ways of Thought in Ancient China* (London: Allen & Unwin, 1939) is a brilliant introduction to the thinking of the Confucian, Taoist, and Legalist schools.

11. See my translation in Penguin Classics, 2002, in which I examine at some length the way Sun-tzu exploits Taoist thinking. The extract comes in Chapter 6, pp. 37–8.
12. See D. C. Lau, tr., *Mencius* (London: Penguin Classics, 1970); Burton Watson, tr., *Hsun-Tzu Basic Writings* (New York: Columbia University Press, 1963); John S. Major et al., trs., *The Huainanzi* (New York: Columbia University Press, 2010); and A. C. Graham, tr., *The Book of Lieh-Tzu* (London: John Murray, 1960).
13. See the translation of this passage by Wing-tsit Chan in John Minford and Joseph Lau, eds., *Classical Chinese Literature: An Anthology of Translations* (New York and Hong Kong: Columbia University and Chinese University of Hong Kong, 2000), pp. 606–7; also another version in Yutang Lin, *The Chinese Theory of Art* (London: Putnam, 1967), pp. 31–3.
14. See the translation by Herbert Giles in Minford and Lau, eds., *Classical Chinese Literature*, pp. 944ff, on which this is based.
15. This is Lin Dai-yu holding forth about music to her cousin Jia Bao-yu, in Chapter 86 of the eighteenth-century novel *The Story of the Stone* (London: Penguin Classics, 1982), p. 154.
16. See the extract from his biography above.
17. Isabelle Robinet, "*Daode jing*," in Fabrizio Pregadio, ed., *The Routledge Encyclopedia of Taoism* (London and New York, 2008), p. 311.
18. See the excellent discussion by D. C. Lau in the Introduction to his translation, *Lao Tzu: Tao Te Ching* (London: Penguin Classics, 1963).
19. These archaeological discoveries have been extensively studied and have led to some fascinating discussions of textual variations and intricacies of early Taoist thought. See for example the two translated versions (1998 and 2000) by Henricks, and the detailed 1998 conference proceedings edited by Sarah Allan and Crispin Williams. See also Dan Murphy's 2006 master's thesis at the University of Massachusetts, Amherst, which is available online. Details of these are all given in Further Reading.
20. Chapters 81, 5, 23, and 2.
21. Chapters 1 and 56, and the River Master's commentary on Chapter 5.
22. Meyer in *The Huainanzi* (2010), p. 872.
23. This is the final sentence of his wise and thought-provoking essay "Reading the 'Daodejing': Ethics and Politics of the Rhetoric," *CLEAR*, vol. 25 (Dec. 2003).
24. Needham, *Science and Civilisation in China*, vol. 2 (Cambridge: Cambridge University Press, 1956), p. 37.
25. Wilhelm, tr., *Tao Te Ching*. English version by H. G. Ostwald (London: Routledge, 1985), p. 69.
26. Chapter 15.
27. Commentaries on Chapter 20, Chapter 41, Magister Liu's Commentary on Chapter 58.
28. Chapter 47, and Magister Liu's Commentary on Chapter 47.
29. An interesting example of this long tradition of Commentary is the recent book by the former (and, after the Tiananmen killings, disgraced) minister of culture, Wang Meng, entitled *Help from Lao-tzu* (Taipei: Maitian, 2012). A passage typical of his straightforward and heartwarming approach is to be found on p. 432: "In all of *The Tao and the Power* the most beautiful lines are 'Ruling a Great Nation is like cooking a Small Fish.' What a wonderfully concise, what a brilliantly pithy, effortlessly beautiful, and clear statement! If only the world's statesmen could hang this on their study walls, if only they could learn not to meddle, but to pay things exactly as much attention as they need, and no more. I'm no scholar, but I concur with this sentiment from the bottom of my heart." The latest compendium of traditional Commentaries, published in China in 2015, runs to fifteen bulky tomes, and contains the work of almost seven hundred Commentators over the ages.
30. From Magister Liu's General Preface. Liu Yiming, *Daodejing Yaoyi*, p. 195 in the *Laozi jicheng* edition.

31. Commentary on Chapter 52.
32. Magister Liu's Commentary on Chapter 6.
33. As recorded in the *Lives of the Immortals*, a collection of tales attributed to the Taoist Master and Alchemist Ge Hong (283–343), known as Baopuzi, "the Master who Embraces Simplicity."
34. Isabelle Robinet, *Taoism: Growth of a Religion*, tr. Phyllis Brooks (Stanford, CA: Stanford University Press, 1997).
35. Cao Xueqin, *The Story of the Stone: Volume One, The Golden Days*, tr. David Hawkes, (London: Penguin Classics, 1973), p. 63.
36. Cao Xueqin and Gao E, *The Story of the Stone: Volume Five, The Dreamer Wakes*, tr. John Minford (London: Penguin Classics, 1986), p. 360.
37. For an excellent introduction to Magister Liu on Internal Alchemy, see his *Cultivating the Tao*, the work translated by Fabrizio Pregadio and listed in Further Reading.
38. Bernhard Karlgren, *The Poetical Parts in Lao-Tsi* (Göteborg, Sweden: Elanders, 1932), p. 7.
39. Waley, Introduction, pp. 96–7.
40. Gerard Manley Hopkins, "God's Grandeur" and "The Windhover."
41. Benjamin Hoff, *The Tao of Pooh* (New York: Penguin, 1982).
42. In his Foreword to the 1962 St. John's University Press reprint of John C. H. Wu's translation, *Tao Teh Ching*, subsequently reissued by Shambhala in 2003.
43. *Science and Civilisation in China*, vol. 5 (Cambridge: Cambridge University Press), p. 65.
44. It was the official Jesuit translators, creators of the eighteenth-century Latin version of the *I Ching*, who described their predecessors, the earlier Figurists, as "*hallucinantes.*"
45. Jean-Pierre Abel-Rémusat, *Mémoire sur la vie et les opinions de Lao-tseu, philosophe chinois du VI siècle avant notre ère*. Mémoires de l'Académie des Inscriptions et Belles Lettres, Imprimerie Royale, Paris 1823.
46. This is all documented in the interesting article by Knut Walf, "Fascination and Misunderstanding: The Ambivalent Western Reception of Daoism," *Monumenta Serica*, vol. 53 (2005).
47. In his *Lao-tsze's Buch vom höchsten Wesen und vom höchsten Gut*, 1910. Quoted by Walf.
48. In Further Reading I give details of some of the more scholarly translations that have been published over the past two decades.
49. Arthur Waley, tr., *The Way and Its Power* (London: Allen & Unwin, 1935) pp. 44–5. The quotation is from the Fourth Chapter of *The Book of Taoist Master Zhuang*.
50. From Graham's *Disputers of the Tao* (Chicago: Open Court, 1989).
51. From Graham's Preface to his translation of *The Book of Lieh-tzu* (Liezi) (London: John Murray, 1960).
52. In the Introduction to his translation of the Han dynasty Commentator Heshang Gong (the River Master), in *Artibus Asiae*, vol. 8, no. 2/4.
53. Isabelle Robinet in *The Routledge Encyclopedia of Taoism* (London: Routledge, 2008), p. 314.
54. Charles Cummings, OCSO, *Monastic Practices* (Collegeville, MN: Cistercian Publications, 2015), pp. 2–3.
55. Chapter 57.
56. Chapter 80.
57. I owe the experience of this stay to the kindness of my friend Brother Nicholas Koss, OSB.
58. Waley's *The Way and Its Power* (1935) remains for me one of the finest translations, and his long introductory essay is still essential reading for anyone interested in early Chinese thought. Duyvendak originally wrote a Dutch translation during the dark years of the Nazi Occupation (*Het Boek van Weg en Deugd*, 1943). After the war, in 1949, he adapted this into both French (*Le Livre de la Voie et de la Vertu*, 1953) and English (*The Book of the Way and Its Virtue*, 1954). He was overly influenced by the scholarly work of Ma Xulun

(1885–1970) and Gao Heng (1900–1986) and tampered unduly with the text. But his comments are very sensible and helpful.

59. Liu combined wide-ranging and rigorous scholarship with the ability to be quite homely and down-to-earth. See for example his long essay "The Essence of Taoism," in *New Excursions from the Hall of Harmonious Wind* (Leiden: Brill, 1984), p. 144: "If you are helping somebody to do charity work at a fete, you are a Taoist. If you watch birds or walk in the bush, you are a Taoist."

60. For these, see Chapter 15 of my *Classical Chinese Literature: An Anthology of Translations.*

61. In his Foreword, mentioned above at note 42.

62. As Tao Yuanming (365–427) so memorably wrote, "Within these things there is a hint of Truth, but when I try to tell it, I cannot find the Words." I thank John Siciliano, Geremie Barmé, and Richard Rigby for taking the time to read this Introduction and for their insightful and helpful comments. I am once again deeply indebted to my friend Liao Hsin-tien for providing the elegant seal-script calligraphy for this book.

SUGGESTIONS FOR FURTHER READING

In Chinese

Laozi jicheng.
A comprehensive and well-produced and punctuated fifteen-volume collection of Editions and Commentaries, from the very earliest (Guodian) to recent times. Beijing: Zongjiao wenhua, 2011. Since just about everything is included in this vast compendium, I shall only add below one or two other odds and ends that I have consulted.

Chen Guying.
Laozi zhuyi ji pingjie.
Many editions and revisions. Translated by Rhett Y. W. Young and Roger Ames as *Lao-tzu: Text, Notes, and Comments*. San Francisco: Chinese Materials Center, 1977. Chen is one of the liveliest and most thoughtful of contemporary Commentators on this book, as he is on the *I Ching*.

He-shang-gong laozi daodejing (The River Master's Commentary).
I have consulted both the Kwang-wen shu-chü facsimile of a Song dynasty edition (Taipei, 1964) and the carefully edited and punctuated edition in *Laozi jicheng*.

Laozi daodejing zhu, with Commentary by Wang Bi.
Commonly referred to as the vulgate, or Received Text. I have mostly followed this, using the Shi-chieh shu-chü facsimile Taipei, twelfth reprinting, 2005.

Li Ling.
Ren wang dichu zou: Laozi tianxia diyi. Hong Kong: Sanlian, 2008.
An interesting edition and Commentary from a prolific scholar teaching at Peking University.

Liu Yiming.
Daodejing huiyi, Daodejing yaoyi.

For these two Commentaries by Magister Liu, I have followed the punctu-
ated texts in *Laozi jicheng*.
Daoshu shi'er zhong (Twelve Books on the Tao).
Often reprinted collection of works on Internal Alchemy by Magister Liu.

In European Languages

Allen, Sarah, and Crispin Williams, eds.
*The Guodian Laozi: Proceedings of the International Conference, Dartmouth
    College, May 1998*. Berkeley: Society for the Study of Early China,
    2000.

Ames, Roger, and David Hall, trs.
Dao De Jing: Making This Life Significant. New York: Ballantine, 2003.
    A modern philosophical reading, in the inimitable Ames and Hall style.

Carus, Paul, tr.
Lao Tze's Tao-Teh-King. Chicago: Open Court, 1898.
    Thought-provoking translation and Commentary, informed by the inter-
    esting theosophical currents of thought of the late nineteenth century.

Chan, Wing-tsit, tr.
The Way of Lao Tzu. New York: Macmillan, 1963.
    Chan is an authority on Neo-Confucianism, and this bias comes through
    in his Commentary.

Chung-yuan, Chang, tr.
Tao: A New Way of Thinking. New York: Harper & Row, 1975.
    A fascinating, if somewhat abstract, interpretation, much influenced by
    Heidegger.

Coutinho, Steve.
An Introduction to Daoist Philosophies. New York: Columbia University
    Press, 2013.

Creel, Herrlee G.
What Is Taoism? Chicago: University of Chicago Press, 1970.

Duyvendak, J. J. L., tr.

Tau-te-tsjing: Het Boek van Weg en Deugd. Arnhem, Netherlands: Van Loghum
   Slaterus, 1942.
Tao Tö King: Le Livre de la Voie et de la Vertu. Paris: Maisonneuve, 1953.
Tao Te Ching: The Book of the Way and Its Virtue. London: John Murray, 1954.
   Duyvendak relies heavily on the earlier work of the Chinese scholars Ma
   Xulun and Gao Heng, who had often allowed themselves to rearrange the
   text quite arbitrarily, and were unable to consult the early versions un-
   earthed decades later at Mawangdui and Guodian. But I have nonetheless
   benefited enormously from his careful textual reading, and from his always sensitive and thoughtful interpretations, which combine Dutch good
   sense with imaginative insight and a broad knowledge of Chinese culture.

Dyer, Wayne W.
Change Your Thoughts, Change Your Life: Living the Wisdom of the Tao. Carls-
   bad, CA: Hay House, 2011.
   One of the more interesting of the many self-help books based on the *Tao
   Te Ching.*

Erkes, Eduard, tr.
"Ho-shang Kung's Commentary on Lao-Tse." *Artibus Asiae*, vol. 8, no. 2/4,
   Ascona, Switzerland: Artibus Asiae, 1958.

Feng, Gia-Fu, and Jane English, trs.
Tao Te Ching. New York: Knopf, 1972.

Giles, Herbert A., tr.
Chuang Tzu, Taoist Philosopher and Chinese Mystic. Revised edition. London:
   Allen & Unwin, 1926.
   This Victorian translation, first published in the late 1880s, greatly im-
   pressed Oscar Wilde, and is still an eloquent introduction to the world of
   Master Zhuang.

Graham, A. C., tr.
The Book of Lieh-tzu. London: John Murray, 1960.
   Fluent translation of *The Book of Taoist Master Lie.*

Graham, A. C.
Disputers of the Tao: Philosophical Argument in Ancient China. Chicago:
   Open Court, 1989.

One of the most scintillating studies of early Chinese thought ever written.

Henricks, Robert G., tr.
Lao-tzu: Te-Tao Ching: A New Translation Based on the Recently Discovered Ma-wang-tui Texts. New York: Ballantine, 1989.
Lao Tzu's Tao Te Ching: A Translation of the Startling New Documents Found at Guodian. New York: Columbia University Press, 2000.

Ivanhoe, Philip J., tr.
The Daodejing of Laozi. New York: Seven Bridges, 2002.

Julien, Stanislaus, tr.
Lao Tseu, Tao Te King. Paris, 1842.
This was the version made by the early French sinologue, as used by Tolstoy.

Karlgren, Bernhard.
"The Poetical Parts in Lao-Tsi." Göteborg, Sweden: Elanders, 1932.
Meticulous reconstruction of the rhymes.

Komjathy, Louis.
Cultivating Perfection: Mysticism and Self-transformation in Early Quanzhen Daoism. Leiden, Netherlands, and Boston: Brill, 2007.
Daoism: A Guide for the Perplexed. London: Bloomsbury Academic, 2014.

Lau, D. C., tr.
Lao Tzu: Tao Te Ching. London: Penguin Classics, 1963. Also various later bilingual editions from the Chinese University Press.

Legge, James, tr.
The Texts of Taoism. Oxford: Clarendon Press, 1891.

Le Guin, Ursula K., with Jerome P. Seaton, trs.
Tao Te Ching: A Book About the Way and the Power of the Way. Boston: Shambhala, 2009.

Liu Yiming
Cultivating the Tao: Taoism and Internal Alchemy, tr. Fabrizio Pregadio. Mountain View, CA: 2013.

An excellent translation of Magister Liu's difficult treatise. Invaluable for readers wishing to delve deeper into the arcane world of *neidan*, or Internal Alchemy, which lies behind Liu's Commentary on *The Tao and the Power*, but which has been largely excluded from the present translation.

Lin Yutang, tr.
The Wisdom of Laotse, 2 vols Chinese-English Bilingual Edition. Taipei: Cheng-chung, 2009.
Lin cleverly accompanies his translation with lengthy extracts from *The Book of Taoist Master Zhuang* (Zhuangzi).

Lynn, Richard John, tr.
The Classic of the Way and Virtue: A New Translation of the Tao-te Ching of Laozi as Interpreted by Wang Bi. New York: Columbia University Press, 1999.

Mair, Victor H., tr.
Tao Te Ching: The Classic Book of Integrity and the Way. New York: Bantam, 1990.

Major, John S., Sarah A. Queen, et al., trs.
Liu An, King of Huainan, *The Huainanzi*, New York: Columbia University Press, 2010.
An impeccable rendering of this vast compendium, containing much Taoist material, and abundant quotations from *The Tao and the Power*.

Maspero, Henri.
Taoism and Chinese Religion. Tr. Frank A. Kierman, Jr. Amherst: University of Massachusetts Press, 1981.
Maspero, son of the renowned Egyptologist Gaston Maspero, died in Buchenwald in 1945. He was one of the last giants of French sinology. This book is still essential reading, placing Taoism in a broad historical and cultural context.

Mathieu, Rémi, tr.
Lao Tseu: Le Daode jing, Classique de la voie et de son efficience. Paris: Entrelacs, 2008.
A very careful rendering that takes into account all the latest archaeological findings. Mathieu is scrupulous about giving varying readings and

interpretations, which makes this a hard text to follow for the layman, but a useful one for the scholar.

Murphy, Dan.
"A comparison of the Guodian and Mawangdui Laozi texts." MA thesis, University of Massachusetts, Amherst, 2006.
  Available online at: http://scholarworks.umass.edu/cgi/viewcontent .cgi?article=2401&context=theses.

Needham, Joseph, and Wang Ling.
Science and Civilisation in China: Volume 2, History of Scientific Thought. Cambridge: Cambridge University Press, 1956.
  Needham's insights are still wide-ranging and powerful, although the Marxist historian of Chinese thought Hou Wailu too frequently led him astray.

Pregadio, Fabrizio, ed.
The Routledge Encyclopedia of Taoism. 2 vols. London: Routledge, 2008.
  A vast compendium of Taoist lore, with contributions from around the globe.

Read, Dan G., tr.
The Ho-Shang Kung Commentary on Lao Tzu's Tao Te Ching. Montreal: Center Ring, 2015.

Robinet, Isabelle.
Les Commentaires du Tao Tö King jusqu'au VIIe siècle. Paris: Presses Universitaires de France, 1977.
Taoism: Growth of a Religion. Tr. Phyllis Brooks. Stanford, CA: Stanford University Press, 1997.

Ryden, Edmund, tr.
Laozi, Daodejing. Oxford: Oxford World's Classics, 2008.
  A fine translation that takes full account of the Mawangdui and Guodian texts.

Schipper, Kristofer, and Franciscus Verellen, eds.
The Taoist Canon, 3 volumes. Chicago: University of Chicago Press, 2004.
  A monumental guide to the enormous treasure house of the *Daozang.*

Schwartz, Benjamin I.
The World of Thought in Ancient China. Cambridge, MA: Belknap, 1985.

Waley, Arthur, tr.
The Way and Its Power: A Study of the Tao Tê Ching and Its Place in Chinese Thought. London: Allen & Unwin, 1934.
Three Ways of Thought in Ancient China. London: Allen & Unwin, 1939.
Contains an excellent sampling of Taoist Master Zhuang.

Watson, Burton, tr.
The Complete Works of Chuang Tzu. New York: Columbia University Press, 1968.
This is still the best translation of the great Taoist mystic.

Watts, Alan.
Tao: The Watercourse Way. New York: Pantheon, 1975.
One of the last books by this gifted popularizer of Chinese mystical thought, author of *The Way of Zen.*

Welch, Holmes.
Taoism: The Parting of the Way. Boston: Beacon Press, 1965.

Wilhelm, Richard, tr.
Das Geheimnis der Goldenen Blüte: Das Buch von Bewusstsein und Leben. English version by Cary F. Baynes, *The Secret of the Golden Flower: A Chinese Book of Life.* London: Routledge and Kegan Paul, 1931.
Lao Tse: Dao De Ging, das klassische Buch vom Sinn und Leben. English translation by H. G. Ostwald, *Tao Te Ching: The Book of Meaning and Life.* London: Routledge, 1985.

Yu, Anthony C.
"Reading the 'Daodejing': Ethics and Politics of the Rhetoric," *CLEAR,* vol. 25 (Dec. 2003).
Despite its off-putting title, this is one of the very best accounts of *The Way and the Power,* filled with the deep thinking one had grown accustomed to expect from this great scholar.

GATEWAY TO ALL MARVELS

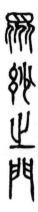

The Tao that can be Told
Is not the True Tao;
Names that can be Named
Are not True Names.
The Origin of Heaven and Earth
Has no Name.
The Mother of the Myriad Things
Has a Name.
Free from Desire,
Contemplate the Inner Marvel;
With Desire,
Observe the Outer Radiance.
These issue from One Source,
But have different Names.
They are both a Mystery.
Mystery of Mysteries,
Gateway to All Marvels.

THE RIVER MASTER

The Tao that can be Told is the mundane Tao of the Art of Government, as opposed to the True Tao of Nature, of the So-of-Itself, of Long Life, of Self-Cultivation through Non-Action. This is the Deep Tao, which cannot be Told in Words, which cannot be Named. The Names that can be Named are such worldly things as Wealth, Pomp, Glory, Fame, and Rank.

> The Ineffable Tao
> Emulates the Wordless Infant,
> It resembles
> The Unhatched Egg,
> The Bright Pearl within the Oyster,
> The Beauteous Jade amongst Pebbles.
> It cannot be Named.

The Taoist glows with Inner Light, but seems outwardly dull and foolish. The Tao itself has no Form, it can never be Named.

> The Root of the Tao
> Proceeds from Void,
> From Non-Being,
> It is the Origin,
> The Source of Heaven and Earth,
> Mother of the Myriad Things,
> Nurturing All-under-Heaven,
> As a Mother Nurtures her Children.

MAGISTER LIU

The single word *Tao* is the very Core of this entire Classic, its lifeblood. Its Five Thousand Words speak of this Tao and of nothing else.

> The Tao itself
> Can never be
> Seen.
> We can but witness it

Inwardly,
Its Origin,
Mother of the Myriad Things.
The Tao itself can never be
Named,
It cannot be Told.

And yet we resort to Words, such as *Origin*, *Mother*, and *Source*.

Every Marvel
Contemplated,
Every Radiance
Observed,
Issues from this One Source.
They go by different Names,
But are part of the same
Greater Mystery,
The One Tao, the Origin, the Mother.
In freedom from Desire,
We look within
And Contemplate
The Inner Marvel,
Not with eyes
But inwardly
By the Light of Spirit.
We look outward
With the eyes of Desire,
And Observe
The Outer Radiance.

Desire itself, in its first Inklings, in the embryonic Springs of Thought, is born within the Heart-and-Mind. Outer Radiance is perceived through Desire, in the World, in the opening and closing of the Doors of Yin and Yang. This is the Named, the Visible, these are the Myriad Things. Thus, both with and without Desire, we draw near to the Mystery of Mysteries, to the Gateway that leads to all Marvels, to the Tao.

)((
)((

John Minford: *The Tao and the Power* says to its reader at the very outset, "Only through experience, only through living Life to the full, in both the Inner and Outer Worlds, can the True Nature of the Tao be Understood and communicated. Not through Words." Desire and the Life of the Senses are part of that experience. Through Desire we witness and enjoy the Beauty of the World, we Observe the Outer Radiance of the Tao. We live Life, we bask in its Radiance. Taoists do not deny the Senses. But Contemplation, the Light of Deep Calm, of meditative experience, goes further. It reveals the Inner Marvel, the Mystery of Mysteries. Outer Radiance and Inner Marvel issue from one and the same Source, which is the Tao. This twofold path is one of the central themes in Magister Liu's commentary, one to which he returns again and again, exhorting the Taoist Aspirant to begin from Observation of the Outer Radiance, and to proceed through Contemplation of the Inner Marvel to a deeper level of Self-Cultivation, to a deeper Attainment of the Tao. "It is Contemplation that gives spiritual significance to objects of sense."

The Book of Taoist Master Zhuang: The Great Tao cannot be Told. The Great Discussion lies beyond Words . . . Where can I find someone who Understands this Discussion beyond Words, who Understands the Tao that can never be Told? This True Understanding of the Tao is a Reservoir of Heaven-and-Nature. Pour into it and it is never full. Pour from it and it is never exhausted. It is impossible to know whence it comes. It is Inner Light.

Arthur Waley: Not only are Books the mere discarded husk or shell of wisdom, but Words themselves, expressing as they do only such things as belong to the normal state of consciousness, are irrelevant to the deeper experience of the Tao, the "wordless doctrine."

Jan Duyvendak: The ordinary, mundane Tao (the one that can be easily Told, or talked about) is unchanging, static, and permanent. The True Tao is Elusive and Ineffable, is in its very Essence Perpetual Change. In the Tao, nothing whatsoever is fixed and unchanging. This is the first great paradox of this Classic, the ever-shifting Cycle of Change, of Being and Non-Being, in which Life and Death constantly yield to and alternate with each other.

Richard Wilhelm: In the Taoist Heart-and-Mind, Psyche and Cosmos are related to each other like the Inner and Outer Worlds.

JM: A Tao that *could* be Told might be any one of the Prescriptions for Living and Ruling that were being proposed in the ferment of the Chinese Warring States period (475–221 BC). All of them would have been called a Tao, a Way, a Recipe for Life. One such Tao, for example, was contained in the little book from that period known as *The Art of War* (*Sunzi bingfa*), whose "author," Sun-tzu (Sunzi), is every bit as lost in the mists of legend as Lao-tzu (Laozi). The Deep Tao, the True Way, and the inexhaustible Inner Power or Strength that flows from the experience of the Tao, are the subjects of this whole Five Thousand Word text. But they are beyond Telling. Words and Names are nothing more than disjointed bits and pieces; they fragment the whole, the One Tao. The paradoxical Mystery of Mysteries is that the Taoist fuses Being on the one hand (the Radiance, Magnificence, and Beauty of the Outer World, as perceived through the Senses, through Desire), and Non-Being on the other (the Dark Intangible Marvel and Mystery of the Inner World). This fusion, this Gateway to Marvels, does not lend itself to any simplistic Name or Label. Names were the preoccupation of more worldly schools of thought, especially the Confucians, for whom Names needed to correspond precisely to Things. As with so much of this short and densely ambiguous Classic, the Chinese word used here for Name, *ming*, has more than one meaning. It also means Fame, Renown, or Reputation (it is after all by being Famous that one acquires a "Name" for oneself). Taoists care nothing for Fame. They hide their Light. They are incognito. And yet, despite these protestations about the vanity of Words and Names, and the powerlessness of Words to describe the True Nature of the Tao, despite the futility of even attempting to define or dissect the Tao, paradoxically, *The Tao and the Power* itself is written in an intensely poetic language (sometimes mesmerizingly and bafflingly so), which edges imperceptibly toward the Wordless Truth; it is an inaudible Song with neither Words nor Music, it sings the Silence that is the Tao. The Tao needs to be experienced, not talked about. This Classic and its countless Commentaries do talk, they propose all manner of Images (see the Taoist Florilegium appended at the end of my translation for a selection of these). But these are merely pointers toward the Tao, toward the gnosis of Taoist experience, parts of a hermetic vocabulary for initiates. In that sense these Names are No-Names.

Arthur Waley, whose translation from the 1930s remains one of the best, gives us a pithy summary of this first Chapter and of the whole book. "In dispassionate Vision the Taoist sees a world consisting of the things for which

A WORDLESS TEACHING

That which All-under-Heaven
Considers
Beautiful
May also be considered
Ugly;
That which All-under-Heaven
Considers
Good
May also be considered
Not-Good.
Being and Non-Being
Engender one another.
Hard and Easy
Complete each other.
Long and Short
Generate each other.
High and Low
Complement each other.
Melody and Harmony

Resonate with each other.
Fore and Aft
Follow one another.
These are Constant Truths.
The Taoist dwells in
Non-Action,
Practices
A Wordless Teaching.
The Myriad Things arise,
And none are rejected.
The Tao gives Birth
But never Possesses.
The Taoist Acts
Without Attachment,
Achieves
Without dwelling
On Achievement,
And so never loses.

THE RIVER MASTER

The Taoist rules through Non-Action, through the Tao. The Taoist guides
through Wordless Teaching, by example. The Primal Breath-Energy of the
Tao gives Life to the Myriad Things, but never Possesses them.

The Tao seeks
No recompense.
The Taoist,
Having Achieved,
Retires to Seclusion
And never dwells on
Achievement.

MAGISTER LIU

Non-Action and Wordlessness are the Core of this Chapter, Freedom from so-called Knowledge. Whosoever goes beyond False Knowledge is freed from "opposites" such as Beautiful and Ugly, High and Low. From this Higher Knowledge flows a Life without Possession or Attachment. The Heart-and-Mind of Opposition (such as that between Beautiful and Ugly) brings a Diminution of Life-Essence, a loss of Spirit, a confusion of Emotion. All of these damage Life. The Taoist abides in Non-Action. Freed from all such distinctions, which melt away in the Taoist Heart-and-Mind, the Taoist Returns to Non-Action, to the Wordlessness that leaves no trace.

> White is contained
> Within Black,
> Light shines
> In an Empty Room.
> This is the Taoist Vision.
> The Taoist finds Joy
> In unalloyed
> Serenity and Calm.

芝

The Book of Taoist Master Zhuang: Every That is also a This, every This is also a That. A thing may not be visible as That, it may be perceived as This. This and That produce each other. Where there is Birth there is Death. Where there is Death there is Birth. Affirmation creates Denial, Denial creates Affirmation. Right creates Wrong, Wrong creates Right. The Taoist's This is also a That, the Taoist's That is also a This.

Waley: The first great principle of Taoism is the relativity of all attributes. Nothing in itself is either long or short. If we call a thing long, we merely mean longer than something else that we take as a standard. What we take as our standard depends on what we are used to . . . All antinomies, not merely high and low, long and short, but Life and Death themselves, merge in the Taoist identity of opposites. The type of the Sage who in true Taoist manner "disappeared" after Achieving Victory is Fan Li (fifth century BC) who, although offered half the kingdom if he would return in triumph with the victorious armies of Yue, "stepped into a light boat and was heard of no more."

The poet Su Dongpo (1037–1101):

> Truest words
> Cannot be spoken.
> Truest sound
> Cannot be heard.
> The tides of the Ocean
> Reach beyond the Mountains,
> The subtlest echoes
> Are deep in the clouds.

NON-ACTION

Not to Honor the Worthy
Puts an end to Contending
Among the folk.
Not to Prize Rare Goods
Puts an end to Theft
Among the folk.
Not to Display Objects of Desire
Removes Chaos
From the Heart-and-Mind
Of the folk.
The Taoist rules by
Emptying Heart-and-Mind
And Filling Belly,
By softening the Will to Achieve,
And strengthening Bones.
The Taoist frees the folk
From False Knowledge and Desire.
Those with False Knowledge
No longer dare to Act.

The Taoist Accomplishes
Through Non-Action,
And all is well Ruled.

THE RIVER MASTER

The Worthy are those who have Achieved High Rank, and have as a consequence become estranged from the Tao, by involving themselves in worldly
affairs. If however they are not publicly rewarded, if they do not receive
Honor and Riches, then ordinary folk are not driven by ambition to emulate
them and strive for Fame and Glory. Instead they can Return to the Calm of
their True Nature. If Rare Goods are not prized in public, then ordinary folk
will not be driven by Greed to Acquire them. If the Ruler returns gold to the
mountains, casts pearls and precious pieces of jade back into the waters of the
Abyss, if the Ruler is pure and uncorrupted, then the common folk will not
feel Greed. The Taoist Rules the Nation as if it were Self, emptying Heart-and-
Mind of Desire, and the folk Eschew Chaos and Confusion. The Taoist Fills
Belly with the Tao, with the One. The Human Heart-and-Mind grows Supple
and Soft. The folk no longer Contend.

The Marrow grows full,
The Bones firm.
Free from False Knowledge
And Desire,
The folk Return
To Calm,
To Simplicity and Purity.
They find Peace
In Non-Action,
In the Rhythms of Nature.

MAGISTER LIU

Once False Knowledge and Desire have been extinguished, once the Worthy
are no longer honored and Rare Goods are no longer prized, then there is

no Contending, no Theft, but instead there is Order, a full Belly, and firm Bones. When the Multitude see such things as Fame and Wealth lying beyond their grasp, they will strive to Acquire them. When rare and highly prized Objects of Desire are put on show, they will steal in order to lay their hands on them.

> The Heart-and-Mind,
> Free of Desire,
> Turns inward
> To True Knowledge,
> To the Knowledge
> That Knows without Knowing.
> Then Action is Eschewed,
> And all is Accomplished
> Through Non-Action,
> Through the Pure Breath-Energy
> Of the Tao.

JM: Confucius advocated Honoring the Worthy. So did Master Mo (the "neglected rival of Confucius," advocate of Universal Love, ca. 470–ca. 391 BC). One whole section of the *Book of Master Mo* is entitled "Honoring the Worthy," and contrasts with this teaching of Lao-tzu:

> This prevalence of poverty, scarcity, and chaos arises because Rulers have failed to Honor the Worthy and to employ the capable in their government. When the Worthy are numerous in the state, Order will be stable; when the Worthy are scarce, Order will be unstable. Therefore the task of the Ruler lies in multiplying the Worthy.

This conventional Honoring of the Worthy was a pillar of the Chinese meritocracy for centuries, and has lasted to the present day, with all of its concomitant ills—an obsession with social status, ambition, corruption, nepotism, and deadening conformity. The Taoist shuns all of this. In an important sense, Non-Action implies Anarchy.

The Taoist Bo Yuchan (1194–1229), Vagabond of the Bohea Hills, describes the Non-Action and Freedom of the Hermit in his poem "Written When Drunk":

> *The Taoist thinks of Heaven and Earth*
> *As Home,*
> *Gazes daily at streams and hills,*
> *Eyes for ever Clear,*
> *Dwells mid moonlit bamboos,*
> *In a poetic Realm,*
> *In the shadows of windswept pines,*
> *In a world of wine . . .*
> *Office may bring*
> *Honor and Renown,*
> *But better by far*
> *The Hermit's simple fare,*
> *And rough homespun.*

4
EMPTY

The Tao is Empty.
But in Practice
Need never be Filled.
The Tao is Fathomless,
Like the Ancestor of the Myriad Things.
Smooth the Edges,
Loosen the Tangles,
Soften the Light,
Merge with the Dust.
The Tao is Crystalline and Still,
It seems to have been here for ever.
I know not whose Child it is,
It seems to have been
Before the Emperors of Old.

THE RIVER MASTER

The Tao is fathomless and unknowable, like Water in a deep Abyss.

The Tao of Non-Action
Loosens
Tangled Roots,
Softens Vision,
Softens the Light,
Merges with the Dust,
With the Multitude,
Not standing aloof.
Be crystalline,
Like the Tao,
Be Calm,
Endure.

I am the Tao. I was here before the Emperors of Old, before Heaven and Earth. I have been here for ever, in Stillness, Not Contending.

MAGISTER LIU

The inexhaustible Depth of the Tao bubbles up from nowhere like a Spring.

It is always Empty, yet contains all within itself. It is Deep and Still. It dwells amongst the Myriad Things but is never subject to them. It is discovered through Self-Cultivation.

Smooth the Harsh Edges
Of Breath-Energy,
Loosen the Tangles
Of Worldly Emotion,
Glow with a Soft
Harmonious Light.
Dwell in the world,
Do not deny it,
Merge with the Dust,
Resonate with outer things,

Be Still
And not entangled.

The Taoist's Heart-and-Mind is the Tao, the Tao is the Taoist's Heart-and-Mind:

Still as Water,
Bright and Clear
As Radiant Sky
And Lustrous Moon,
Outer Radiance
Containing Inner Marvel.

The *Xiang-er* Commentator: The Edges are the Twisted Designs of Heart-and-Mind. The Tangles are Emotions such as Anger. Every Twisted Design must be made smooth, every Tangle must be loosened as soon as it arises, must never be allowed to reach the Vitals. Harm, even Death, may result. To soften the Light is to Still Emotion.

Waley: Dust is a common Taoist metaphor for the noise and fuss of everyday life.

Wing-tsit Chan: Taoism in its true sense calls for identification with, not an escape from, the world ("merging with the Dust").

Duyvendak: The Tao is portrayed as an Empty Vessel that is never Filled, a reservoir that, therefore, may potentially contain everything, a fathomless depth for all phenomena.

For the Taoist Bo Yuchan, the Observation of Nature and of its ever-changing Countenance serves to deepen Self-Cultivation, Understanding of the Tao.

I built my hut deep in the mountains,
To watch the Myriad Things in Stillness,
Green moss sealing the dawn clouds,

Blue creepers binding the evening moon.
Songbirds hang from the crags,
Dark waters cleanse the bones of rocks.
A wind stirs the mountains like thunder,
The ocean churns waves like snow . . .

THE BELLOWS

Heaven and Earth are not Kind.
They treat the Myriad Things
As Straw Dogs.
Taoists are not Kind,
They treat ordinary folk
As Straw Dogs.
The space between Heaven and Earth
Is like a Bellows,
Empty but never exhausted.
The more it is worked,
The more issues forth from it.
Many Words are soon spent.
Hold Fast to the Center.

THE RIVER MASTER

The Taoist Nurtures the Myriad Folk, not with Kindness, but according to the Laws of Nature, emulating Heaven and Earth, emulating the Harmonious Breath-Energy of the Tao which circulates in the Empty Space between Heaven and Earth, through which the Myriad Things are Born. A Bellows is Empty, but nonetheless produces a Resounding Breath.

> Cast off Passion,
> Moderate Desire,
> Cherish the Purity
> Of a Bright Spirit.
> Much Business
> Harms the Spirit,
> Many Words
> Harm the Person.
> If the mouth keeps opening,
> If the tongue keeps wagging,
> Misfortune will surely follow.

MAGISTER LIU

Hold Fast to the Center, forget Words, Nurture Breath-Energy, be at Peace with Nature, with the So-of-Itself, be Calm and Still. Resonate, Connect, and you will attain to the Greater Kindness. Like Air from a Bellows, Infinite Breath-Energy issues from the Emptiness of the Tao.

> Between Heaven and Earth,
> The Bellows is
> The Tao of Non-Action,
> The Wordless Tao,
> The Tao of Emptiness.

The *Xiang-er* Commentator: Pure Breath-Energy is invisible. It seems Empty, and yet when breathed in and out, it is inexhaustible. In the same way, the more an Empty Bellows is pumped, the more issues from it. Much Learning, like many Words, is ephemeral. Those who do not Cultivate the Tao, who do not keep their Person Whole, will be exhausted at the end of their life-span. Better Hold Fast to the Tao of the Center, the Tao of Harmony.

Duyvendak: Kindness is not a quality inherent in Heaven and Earth. In the processes of Nature, every thing and every being is treated with utter ruthlessness. Confucius in the *Confucian Analects*, XVII:19: "I prefer not to speak . . . Does Heaven speak? The Four Seasons pursue their courses, and all things are continually being produced, but does Heaven ever *say* anything?" Kindness or Benevolence (*ren*), the prime Confucian virtue, is here being challenged. Nature, the So-of-Itself, and hence the Tao, is not Benevolent. On the contrary it is utterly ruthless. Straw dogs (*chugou*) are an image of ruthlessness. They were used as sacrificial offerings in ancient China. During the sacrifice itself they were treated with ceremonial reverence, but once they had been used, they were thrown away and trampled on.

The Neo-Confucian philosopher Zhu Xi (1130–1200) subscribed to many basic Taoist ideas. Take for example this short poem, "A Hermit Seeking Purity":

> *At the dawn window,*
> *Forest shadows unfurl.*
> *From the night pillow,*
> *Mountain springs are heard.*
> *In this seclusion,*
> *There is no more searching.*
> *It is Wordless,*
> *This Heart-and-Mind of the Tao.*

THE VALLEY SPIRIT

The Valley Spirit never Dies.
The Mystic Feminine,
The Gate of the Mystic Feminine,
The Root of Heaven and Earth,
Like a soft silken fiber,
Can be used without end.

MAGISTER LIU

Now we come to the Spirit itself. Consider two mountain peaks facing each other, and the Valley between.

> A voice calls out,
> An echo replies,
> A Sound
> From Nothing,
> A Something
> Without Form,
> Neither a Nothing
> Nor a Something,
> A concentration
> Of Pure Breath-Energy.
> This is the Valley Spirit.

In the Center of Emptiness it dwells, a True Void, a Calm, which both moves and yet is Still. This is the Gate of the Primordial Yang and of the Mystic Feminine Yin, the Gate through which Yin and Yang come and go. Embrace this Valley, never let it out of Heart-and-Mind. This Essence, this Spirit, will Endure, it will never die.

> Wheresoever
> This Spirit is,
> There is the Tao.
> Wheresoever
> It stretches its hand,
> Left and Right,
> It plucks the Fruit,
> The Treasure
> Of Life-Destiny.

To Know the Spirit of the Valley, seek guidance from a True Teacher. Without such a Teacher, all is vain speculation, and the Spirit remains elusive.

Waley: This Chapter may belong to the general stock of early Taoist rhymed teaching.

The *Xiang-er* Commentator: Man should model himself on the Earth, on the Feminine, on Woman, and not be assertive. The Dark Female, the Mystic Feminine, is Earth. The Yin Grotto is the Vagina, the Gate, the Valley, the Essence, the Root of Woman. The Penis is the Root of Man.

JM: The contemporary Peking scholar Li Ling concurs with this sexual interpretation, while Wing-tsit Chan follows the more symbolic (and coy) reading of the Song dynasty Neo-Confucian Master Zhu Xi: "The Valley and the Feminine, like Infant and Water, are Lao-tzu's favorite symbols for the Tao. There is nothing mysterious about the Valley or the Valley Spirit. It simply stands for Emptiness, for vastness, openness, all-inclusiveness, and lowliness or humility. In the words of Zhu Xi, the Valley in itself is Empty. As sound reaches it, it echoes. This is the spontaneity of Spiritual Transformation. The Feminine is that which receives and produces things."

Duyvendak: The Valley and the Gate of the Mystic Feminine are part of the many-layered language of the Taoist initiate, images in the Taoist hermetic vocabulary. The word *pin*, here translated as Feminine, properly designates a female horse or Mare. It has connotations of the docility (but also the power) of a Mare, and of Calm, and is one of the prime qualities of the Tao. In the *I Ching*, the Mare is the principal image of the second Hexagram, *Kun*, Earth.

This is the Steadfastness of a Mare that roams the boundless Earth, Mother of the Myriad Things, Root and Garden of Life, Perfect and Receptive Void, vast capacity. It is Soft and Yielding, it gives Birth and Nurtures, it stores and serves, it goes with the Flow. It is ever present in the Cycle of Birth, Growth, and Death.

Li Bo (701–762), the Drunken Immortal, evokes something of the Valley Spirit in his famous quatrain "The Mountain and I":

> *The birds have flown away,*
> *A cloud floats idly by.*
> *We never tire of looking at each other,*
> *The mountain and I.*

FORE AND AFT

Heaven and Earth last,
They Endure.
They do not give Birth
To other Heavens,
To other Earths.
They Endure.
The Taoist puts Self Aft,
And Self is Fore,
Treats Self as a thing outside,
And Self Endures,
Treats Self as a thing Not-Personal,
And Person is Fulfilled.

THE RIVER MASTER

Heaven and Earth Endure, in Peace and Calm. They give and expect no return. They do not strive to enrich themselves nor do they use Others for their
own ends. They do not beget other Heavens and other Earths, and yet they
are infinitely long-lived. Emulating Heaven and Earth, the Taoist puts Others
first and Self last, is Sparing toward Self and Generous to Others. The Taoist
has no personal goals, and yet the Taoist's Person is Fulfilled Of-Itself.

MAGISTER LIU

Like the Valley Spirit, Heaven and Earth never Die, they are the most lasting
and imperishable things in the entire Universe. They have no goal, no intention to prolong Life. Heaven is Silent, and yet each Season unfolds according
to its appointed time. Earth has no Intention of Heart-and-Mind, and yet the
Myriad Things come into Being. When their time comes, they are Born, they
grow, they are harvested and stored, each according to its Nature. All comes
to pass according to the Season and the Nature of Things. Heaven and Earth
have no Intention to give Birth to other Heavens and other Earths. They are
Empty. Their very Emptiness gives them Long Life. The Taoist, like Heaven
and Earth, Resonates freely with All-under-Heaven, dulls the edge of Cleverness, and Eschews False Knowledge. The Taoist puts Self Aft, and yet True
Self comes effortlessly to the Fore, through Humility and Self-Effacement.
This is the Perfection of the Tao.

Duyvendak: Heaven and Earth generate a multitude of other things, but they
do not reproduce themselves, they do not create other Heavens or Earths.
They show no special concern for their own continued existence, and for this
very reason they Endure. So it is with the Taoist, who has no thought for Self,
who practices Non-Action, who makes no active effort to further Personal
interests. Without any special effort on the Taoist's part, the Tao brings to the
Fore what is Aft, what is there quietly in the background.

Su Dongpo (1037–1101) captures something of the effortless abandonment of Self in these lines from his poem "Crossing Dayu Range":

In a flash
Every impurity is gone,
Body and Mind
Are clean and calm—
This vast feeling,
Alone,
Upright,
Between Heaven and Earth.
Today
High above the range,
Self and World are utterly forgotten,
Hair floats free,
Long Life is assured.

WATER

The Best is like Water.
Water Benefits the Myriad Things.
Water does not Contend.
It abides in that
Which the Multitude abhor.
It is close to the Tao.
The Best Dwelling
Depends on Terrain,
Best Heart-and-Mind
Depends on Depth.
Friendship on Kindness,
Words on Good Faith,
Government on Order,
Practical Matters on Competence,
Movement on Timing.
Wheresoever there is no Contending,
There is no Fault.

THE RIVER MASTER

In Heaven, Water forms mist and falling dew. On Earth it forms springs and lakes. The Multitude abhor the low-lying, abhor all that is damp and muddy. But Water Flows quietly through these very places and settles in them.

> Dammed,
> It comes to a Halt.
> Released,
> It Flows,
> It follows and obeys.
> This is its Nature.
> None can find fault
> With Water.

In its Nature it is close to the Tao. It brings Benefit to plants, Flowing beneath them. It Resembles the Woman lying beneath the Man.

MAGISTER LIU

Through Not-Contending, Water Benefits the Myriad Things. Therein lies its Excellence. True Excellence (in dwelling, in Heart-and-Mind, in friendship, in Words) Resembles Water, which never Contends. Not-Contending is Non-Action, it is the Inner Power of the Tao, which resembles Water. The Multitude prize the high and abhor the low, but the Taoist abides in that which the Multitude abhor and is thereby close to the Tao. In Depth, the Heart-and-Mind finds Calm and Freedom from Desire, just as Water finds Calm in a still, unruffled pond. Just as Water brings moisture to every place, so too the Taoist sees all as equals, close friends, and distant persons alike. The Taoist brings Peace to the elderly, Cherishes the young. The Taoist follows the Promptings of the Heart-and-Mind without ever committing a fault or transgression. [In this last sentence Magister Liu is paraphrasing the *Confucian Analects*.]

Waley: Even ordinary people realize the importance of the Taoist principle of "water-like" behavior, i.e., not striving to get on top or to the fore. This lyrical, almost ecstatic acceptance of the Universal Laws of Nature has inspired some of the most moving passages in Taoist literature.

Li Bo finds Calm in the mountains.

> *You ask me why I dwell in the green mountains.*
> *I smile and make no reply.*
> *My heart is free of care.*
> *The peach-tree blooms,*
> *The waters Flow*
> *Into the unknown.*
> *I dwell in a Realm*
> *That is not of Men.*

LETTING GO

Letting Go is better
Than Filling to the Brim.
A blade overly sharpened
Does not last long.
Halls stuffed with gold and jade
None can preserve.
Wealth, Rank, Pride,
All bring Calamity.
The Tao of Heaven-and-Nature
Is to Accomplish
And to Withdraw.

THE RIVER MASTER

Whosoever Achieves Fame and fails to Withdraw, whosoever does not Let Go, but remains stuck in the place of Honor and Glory, will surely meet with Harm. The Taoist follows the Cycle of the Tao, of Heaven-and-Nature.

> The sun declines
> From its zenith,
> The moon waxes
> Only to wane,
> Flowers bloom
> Only to fade,
> The greatest joy
> Turns to sorrow.

MAGISTER LIU

That which is Filled to the Brim will spill. That which is overly sharpened will break. Such extremes bring their own downfall. Eschew them. No one can hold on to Wealth for ever.

> The Taoist Returns
> To the Root,
> Witnesses the Outer Radiance
> At its height,
> The Full and the Sharp,
> Wealth and Prosperity,
> Then Retreats within
> To Self-Cultivation,
> Frees Self
> From Desire,
> Contemplates
> The Inner Marvel,
> Nourishes
> The Embryo Pearl,
> Safe from Calamity.

This is the Tao of Heaven-and-Nature. This is the Cycle of the Tao. When Grandeur (the auspicious Eleventh Hexagram of the *I Ching*, ☷☰) reaches its Limit of Transformation, when all of its Lines Change, when every one of its three Yang Lines Changes to Yin, and every one of its three Yin Lines Changes to Yang, then Obstruction (the inauspicious Twelfth Hexagram, ☰☷) is Born. And vice versa. The one cannot exist without the other. This is the alternation and evolution of Change, the Cycle of Yin and Yang.

To withdraw
Into Retirement
In the wake of
Accomplishment and Success,
To Let Go,
Averts Calamity.

Duyvendak: Just as one should never keep on filling a vase, or sharpening a blade, so one should never try to hold on to worldly treasures, or boast of Wealth and Rank. The Tao Lets Go, lets things follow their natural course, lets things unfold. Once something is Accomplished, the inevitable Cycle begins again.

Liu Ling (221–300), one of the original Seven Sages of the Bamboo Grove, and another famous drinker, knew how to "let go."

> Often, under the influence of wine, Liu Ling would behave in a completely free and unrestrained manner, sometimes even stripping off his clothes and sitting stark naked in the middle of his room. Once, when others saw him in this state and chided him for it, Ling famously retorted, "Heaven and Earth are my pillars and roof, my house and its rooms are my trousers and jacket. Pray, what are you gentlemen doing in my trousers?"

THE INFANT

Nourish Spirit,
Embrace the One.
Can you keep it
Ever present?
Can you Concentrate
Breath-Energy
To utmost Softness,
Can you be an Infant?
Can you cleanse
The Mystic Vision,
Till it is without spot?
Can you Cherish the folk,
Can you Rule the Nation
Through Non-Action?
Can you open and close
The Gates of Heaven-and-Nature,
And be Woman?
Can you view the Four Quarters
With Utmost Clarity,
With No-Knowledge?

The Tao Begets and Nurtures,
The Tao gives Birth
But never Possesses.
The Taoist Acts
Without Attachment,
Leads but never takes charge.
This is Mystic Power.

THE RIVER MASTER

Whosoever Embraces the One Endures for ever.

The One spreads its Glory
Throughout All-under-Heaven.
The One enters
The Heart-and-Mind,
Then issues forth,
Spreading Inner Power abroad.

With Concentrated Breath-Energy, with Gentleness and Clarity, the Person Resonates and Flows, is Soft and Pliant like an Infant, and Spirit is ever present. To cleanse the Mystic Vision is to purify Heart-and-Mind, is to see with Clarity, deep in the Dark Well of Mystery.

The Taoist,
Like Woman,
Is Quiet and Still,
Soft and Tender.
The Taoist Ruler of a Nation
Is Gentle,
Never Meddles.

MAGISTER LIU

This is the Tao of the Deep Inner Marvel, of the Infant, Embracing the One, Attaining Mystic Power, Mystic Vision. The Human Heart-and-Mind is in Constant Peril, but the Heart-and-Mind of the Tao Endures. The Human Heart-and-Mind is divided, but the Heart-and-Mind of the Tao, of the Infant, is One. There is no Two in it, no Division, no False Knowledge, only the Primordial Power of the Ancients.

> In the Greater Knowledge
> Which resembles
> Folly,
> In the Greater Cleverness
> Which resembles
> Clumsiness,
> Lies the path
> To a Higher Heart-and-Mind,
> To the Inner Power
> Of the Tao.

To Cultivate this Power is to go beyond Attachment and Action, to the Heart-and-Mind of the Tao.

> The Mystic Power
> Of the Infant
> Cannot be seen,
> Cannot be heard,
> Has no Form,
> Leaves no Trace.

Waley: This Chapter on the Infant and the Mystic Power may be an old Taoist hymn which the author here adapts to his own use. The opening passage (on Concentrating Breath-Energy) probably deals with Taoist yoga. Embracing the One, in Quietist language, has a metaphysical sense, meaning to "hold fast to" the One as opposed to the Many, to utilize the primal, "undivided" state that underlies normal consciousness.

Duyvendak: Opening and Closing the Gates of Heaven-and-Nature may be a reference to the Life of the Senses. This Chapter refers to the Yogic art of maintaining Vital Energy, something described more fully in *The Book of Taoist Master Zhuang.*

For the poet Xie Lingyun (385–433), hiking excursions in the mountains were both a form of physical exertion and metaphors for Self-Cultivation, for Embracing the One.

I packed provisions,
Took up my light staff,
And tramped the long and winding way
To my hidden abode . . .
Here I shall live in Peace,
Hold Fast to the One,
Let Calm and Wisdom fuse.
From this day forth,
My Spirit will begin to heal.

NON-BEING

Thirty Spokes joined in a hub
Form a Wheel.
The Emptiness between,
The Non-Being,
Makes the Carriage Useful.
Clay kneaded
Forms a Pot.
The Emptiness within,
The Non-Being,
Makes the Pot Useful.
Windows and doors chiseled
Create a House;
The Emptiness within,
The Non-Being,
Makes the House Useful.
Being and Substance
Bring Benefit.
Non-Being and Emptiness
Make things Useful.

THE RIVER MASTER

Through Doors and Windows, Empty in themselves, we leave and enter, through them we see. The House, Empty in itself, provides lodging, can be lived in. This Usefulness consists in Emptiness, in Non-Being. The Tao itself is Empty.

MAGISTER LIU

The Mystic Power of the Tao, of the One, its Non-Being, make it Useful. Being has its Root in Non-Being. Non-Being is contained within Being. The four limbs and the hundred joints together form a Body, just as the thirty spokes join in a hub to form a Wheel. Flesh and blood, skin and bones, create the Substance of the Human Form, just as Clay forms the Pot. But it is the Seven Apertures or Orifices (ears, nostrils, eyes, and mouth) and the Emptiness within that enable us to Resonate with the outer world, just as it is windows and doors and the Emptiness within that make a House Useful.

Duyvendak: Indispensable though the Spokes may be to form a Wheel, what really matters is the hollow axle. Indispensable though Clay may be for moulding a Pot, the empty space within is what really concerns us. Indispensable though the fashioning of Doors and Windows may be in building a House, the chief thing is the space within. What "is not," therefore, is more important in these cases than "what is."

The Rites of Zhou (Zhouli): The square undercarriage of the ritual coach represents Earth. The round dais represents Heaven. The wheels with their thirty spokes represent sun and moon.

Wang Ji (767–ca. 830) meditates deeply on Being and Non-Being:

> *I traveled a thousand years*
> *Into the past,*

Pondered the Beginning
Of the Myriad Things,
Commanded Non-Being
To become Being,
Watched Substance
Become Void . . .
To the Master of Non-Action I say:
"You are the one
Who Understands All!"

BELLY, NOT EYES

The Five Colors
Blind the eyes.
The Five Sounds
Deafen the ears.
The Five Tastes
Deaden the palate.
The Hunt for Game,
The Heat of the Chase,
Cause Heart-and-Mind
To Run Riot.
Goods that are hard to come by
Become an Impediment.
The Taoist lives through
Inner Nourishment of the Belly,

Not through the eyes,
Eschews the latter,
Chooses the former.

THE RIVER MASTER

Whosoever lusts after Sensual Beauty injures Spirit. Whosoever takes undue pleasure in the Five Sounds becomes deaf to True Harmony, and the Heart-and-Mind can no longer hear the Pure Sound of Silence. Whosoever delights over much in the Five Tastes deadens the palate and loses the True Flavor of the Tao. Spirit thrives on Clarity and Calm, and is Perturbed by the hunting and panting of the Chase. Unbridled Desire for gold and silver, for pearls and jade, injures and degrades.

MAGISTER LIU

The Benefits of Being, of seeing with the Eyes, of hearing with the Ears, of tasting with the Mouth and thinking with the Heart-and-Mind, of walking with the Legs, all of these must be tempered and informed by the Inner Governing Spirit of Non-Being. The Taoist lives through Inner Nourishment of the Belly, through Moderation, not in the unbridled Pleasure of the Senses. It is the Eyes that cause greatest Harm. When Eyes see, then Ears, Mouth, Heart-and-Mind, Limbs are all affected by that stimulus. But if the Eyes are denied sight, then the Five Colors cannot enter. The Taoist Nourishes Breath-Energy in the Dark of the Belly, sees the Inner Marvel within the Outer Radiance. The Taoist Eschews the Light of the Eyes, sees the Color that is No-Color, hears the Sound that is No-Sound, tastes the Taste that is No-Taste.

Waley: This Chapter is an answer to the Chinese Hedonists. Any attempt to enjoy the Senses without restraint, merely leads to a dulling of those Senses. The Belly in this instance means "what is inside," the Inner Power. To

"Eschew the latter" is to Eschew the World of the Senses, to "choose the former" is to choose the Power within.

The poet Tao Yuanming (365–427) was a gentle soul, fond of wine ("the thing in the cup") but not in the flamboyant manner of the Seven Sages of the Bamboo Grove. He was quietly content to "pluck chrysanthemums by the eastern hedge, and gaze afar toward the southern hills." Lin Yutang (1895–1976), himself a fine translator of *The Tao and the Power*, described Tao Yuanming as "the most perfectly harmonious and well-rounded character in the entire Chinese literary tradition." Tao's reflections on Death express a characteristic Calm.

Let Go,
Float
On the Great Transformation,
With neither Joy
Nor Fear.
When it's all over
It's over.
Brooding
Serves no purpose.

NO SELF

Favor and Disgrace
Both Perturb.
Honor and Rank
Bring Great Calamity to Self.
Favor Perturbs
From Above,
Disgrace
From Below.
Gain and Loss
Both Perturb.
I suffer Great Calamity
From Honor and Rank
Because I have a Self.
With No Self,
There is No Calamity.
Whosoever Cherishes
All-under-Heaven
As Self
Can take charge of
All-under-Heaven;
Whosoever Loves

All-under-Heaven
As Self
Can be Trusted with
All-under-Heaven.

THE RIVER MASTER

To win Honor is to enter the Realm of Fear. Whosoever Achieves Rank and
Honor should beware of Pride. Whosoever acquires Wealth should beware of
Extravagance. I fear Calamity because I have a Self. With No-Self, what is
there to fear?

Without Self,
I Attain the Tao
With Ease,
Soaring lightly
Through the clouds,
Roaming freely
To and fro
In the Space
Which is No-Space.
My Spirit
Communes with the Tao.
What Calamity
Can befall me then?

MAGISTER LIU

With No-Self, there is nothing to Honor or Exalt. Favor and Disgrace can
bring no Calamity. This is to place Self Aft, to think of Self as a thing outside.
With no False Knowledge in the Belly, True Breath-Energy is Nourished. If
the Eyes see, the Heart-and-Mind Runs Riot. The Multitude see Favor as De-
sirable, see Disgrace as Perturbing. They fail to Understand that the two are
closely linked, that they depend on each other. Where there is Favor there is

also Disgrace. And vice versa. Both Perturb. High Rank brings Great Calamity. After the zenith comes the descent to the nadir. After Favor, beware of Loss of Favor. If it has been granted, beware lest it be taken away. The True Tao, the Tao that is Safe from Calamity, from both Gain and Loss, is the Tao of No-Self.

Waley (quoting Master Guan): Throw open the gates, bide in silence, and the Radiance of Spirit shall come in and make its home.

JM: The Cycle of Favor and Disgrace was an inescapable feature of life, in a society where every educated individual sat the examinations to enter the public service and climb the ladder of officialdom. The Taoist, through Seclusion and Self-Cultivation in the Tao, through Cultivation of No-Self, aspired to Attain Freedom from this Cycle, from the vicissitudes of public life.

Xi Kang (223–262) of the Bamboo Grove fraternity wrote of his own quest for Calm.

> *Wisdom and learning I abhor:*
> *Wander, my soul, in Quietude!*
> *Wisdom and Learning I detest,*
> *In Quietude I set my rest:*
> *Repenting what may be amiss,*
> *All my ambition, all my bliss,*
> *To trail my hook by some ravine,*
> *Lord of a kingdom quite unseen.*
> *And so, bare-headed as I go,*
> *Though all around are scenes of woe,*
> *This be my song for evermore:*
> *Wander, my soul, in quietude!*

Xi Kang himself fell foul of the ruling Sima clan. But famously, in true Taoist fashion, when Calamity struck, he strummed his Lute all the way to the execution ground.

THE INEFFABLE TAO

Look,
And you never can see it—
It is too Subtle.
Listen,
And you never can hear it—
It is too Faint.
Feel for it,
And you never can take hold of it—
It is too Elusive.
These three
Merge into the One,
They form
The Ineffable Whole
Of the Tao.
There is
No Realm of Brilliance
Above it,
No Realm of Darkness

Beneath,
Just Strand upon Strand
Of the Tao,
Unnameable,
Returning to Non-Matter,
Form without Form,
Ineffable Image
Without Substance.
Greet it,
And its Front cannot be seen.
Follow it,
And its Rear is invisible.
Attain Mastery
Of Present Being
By Understanding
The Tao of Old.
To Understand
The Ancient Beginning
Is the Binding Strand
Of the Tao.

THE RIVER MASTER

The Subtle Color and Sound of the Tao cannot be Told, they must be absorbed in the Simple Calm of Spirit, when Emotion and Desire have been Stilled.

MAGISTER LIU

An Understanding of the Ancient Beginning is Attained through Primal Breath-Energy, when all that is Elusive, Faint, and Subtle is merged into One Inner Vision of the Whole. This is to Understand Ultimate Reality, Non-Being in the Myriad Beings of the Present.

This Understanding
Is the Binding Strand
Of the Tao,
Strand upon Strand,
Countless Transformations,
Of Being
Returning to Non-Being,
In the Flow of Nature,
Returning
To the One with No Substance
Which dwells in its midst,
To the Ancient Beginning
That Binds.

Waley: "Not seen," etc. is the traditional description of ghosts and spirits, adopted here as a description of the shadowy Tao. To "Understand the Ancient Beginning" has a double sense—macrocosmically, in the Universe, and microcosmically, in oneself. The Binding Strand is literally the "main thread" of the Tao.

Duyvendak: The Tao operates imperceptibly in all phenomena, too numerous to be defined by Names, until it Returns to Non-Being. One never meets it face to face.

Zhu Xi, in his poem "In my Studio," writes of the Calm of Seclusion, in which such an Understanding of the Beginning can be Attained.

Men of the World
Pursue their personal views,
Parade their Wisdom,
And so the Tao grows dim.
Hermits of the forest,
Different by far,
Seek in Seclusion
The Beginning
Of the Myriad Transformations.

DARKLY CONNECTED

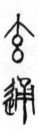

Of Old
Taoists were
Subtle and Marvelous,
Darkly Connected,
Deep beyond all Knowing.
Since they could never be Known,
Let us tell
How they seemed:
Hesitant,
As though
Crossing a stream in winter,
Apprehensive,
As though
Fearing neighbors on all sides.
Cautious,
Like Guests;
Melting,
Like Ice at first Thaw;
Simple,
Like a Block of Uncarved Wood;
Broad as a Valley,
Murky as Mud,
Mud that settles and clears.

Who can Attain Calm
And live in Gentle Motion?
The Taoist has no
Craving for Plenitude,
But remains Unfilled,
Worn and Incomplete.

THE RIVER MASTER

The Taoists of Old were Darkly Connected with Heaven-and-Nature, they were imbued with the Mysterious Essence.

To others they seemed
Blind and deaf.
None knew their Inner Power.
They seemed Cautious
Like guests,
Wary of causing offense,
And yet they were
Broad and Open as a Valley.
They were Empty,
Not Craving Honor and Fame.
They Embraced all.
They mixed with the Multitude
And were not aloof.

Murky Water settles quietly, it slowly becomes Clear. Calm quickens gently. The Tao has no Desire for Plenitude or Abundance, has no need to be Perfect.

MAGISTER LIU

The Taoists of Old were content to be Worn and Incomplete:

To be Simple and Broad,
Murky,

Like Mud settling,
Gradually Attaining Calm.
They were
Subtle and Hidden,
Marvelously Themselves
Of-Themselves.

Many Taoists of today have lost the Primordial Tao of Before-Heaven, have
lost the True Countenance of the Ancient Beginning.

They are
Muddy and unclear,
They are
Neither peaceful nor lively.
To Attain Clarity and Calm,
To Purify the Human Heart-and-Mind,
Is to be Alive,
Is to Witness
The Quickening
Of the Heart-and-Mind of the Tao,
The Return of the Real.

Duyvendak: The Taoists of Old were hesitant, circumspect, reserved, melting, not firm practical men of Action. They did not behave in an artificial,
contrived manner. They were solid and authentic, like the Uncarved Block.
They were broad and comprehensive in their ideas. They may have seemed
"murky," but through Non-Action and Calm they knew how to Transform
Murk into Clarity. They always ended in the Calm of Non-Action. They Eschewed Plenitude, that is to say, they made no effort to take matters to the
fullest stage of development. Instead they let the Law of Constant Change
operate within themselves, which may have meant Diminution rather than
Plenitude.

In his "Rhapsody on Living in the Mountains," Xie Lingyun aspires to the
Dark Connection of the Taoists of Old.

I drink
From the Springs of Antiquity,
I Cherish
The deep Purity of the mountains.
I bid farewell
To the pretty pagodas of cities,
I flee
From the world of towns.
Joyfully I gaze
Upon Simplicity,
Embrace
The Uncarved Block.
Truly Sweet Dew is to be found here
In this Place of Illumination.

RETURN TO THE ROOT

Attain Utmost Emptiness,
Purest Calm.
The Myriad Things arise.
I watch their Return,
Each thing in the World's Profusion
Returning to its Root,
Its True Life-Destiny.
The Return to Root is
Calm.
The Return to Destiny is
Constancy.
With Constancy
There is Light,
Without Constancy
Delusions and Calamity arise.
Constancy is
Acceptance,
Acceptance is
To be Noble,
To be Whole,
One with Heaven-and-Nature,
With the Enduring Tao.

With No-Self
There is no Harm.

THE RIVER MASTER

From Clarity and Calm
Within,
From Utmost Emptiness and Simplicity,
I watch the Myriad Things
Return
To their Root.
The Root is
Soft and Pliant.
To Return to Life-Destiny
Is to walk Constantly in the Tao,
In the Light,
In Calm.

Without the Constancy of the Tao, all manner of Misfortunes arise, and Spirit suffers. The Constancy of the Tao is an All-Embracing Acceptance, it is to abandon Emotion and to forget Desire, to be Noble and Whole.

It is to be Connected
With All-under-Heaven,
To be lasting,
To Endure,
To be
No longer vulnerable to Harm.

MAGISTER LIU

With Emptiness and Calm, the Myriad Things are seen to arise Of-Themselves, Life is seen to unfold of its own accord, in the So-of-Itself. This is the Return to the Root, to Life-Destiny. Acceptance of Imperfection is Attained through

Utmost Emptiness and Purest Calm, through the Return to the Primal, to the
Root. All Vain Thoughts vanish, all Cares fade away.

From the Emptiness
Of Non-Being,
The Mystic Pearl
Crystallizes
In effortless Transformation,
Seen not with Eyes
But with Spirit,
In Inner Silence.

With the Return to the Primal, to the Root, to where Non-Being and Being
are One again, the World's Hurly-Burly grows quiet.

White Light shines
In an Empty Room,
The Inner Marvel
Of Illumination,
Born of Outer Radiance.

With this Embryo, the Mystic Pearl, the Great Tao is Born. The Myriad
Things are seen as One, the distinction between Self and Others fades away.
The Heart-and-Mind is the Tao, the Tao is the Heart-and-Mind. They are One
Reality. The Tao is Immortal, I too am Immortal, a Diamond, an Enduring
Adamantine Substance. The Illusory Self is no more, the True Self is Born,
which neither tiger nor rhinoceros can Harm, which can be hurt by neither
sword nor lance.

With the Death of Self,
In the Transformation
Of Emptiness and Calm,
The Tao does not Die,
But Lives.

Duyvendak: The Cycle whereby things Flourish and Decay is a Truth which one only fully Understands by becoming Empty of Self, and Calm. Then all phenomena Return to the Origin from which they came. Acceptance of this is a Surrender to Life-Destiny. If one does not Understand this Constant Law of Rise and Decline, if one foolishly tries to perpetuate a certain state of affairs, if one goes against the natural unfolding of things, this can only bring Harm. But with this Understanding, one is in Harmony with the Tao, and one can survive even Ruin.

Zheng Banqiao (1693–1765), one of the Eight Eccentrics of Yangzhou, saw a "mindless" Block of Stone as a symbol of Calm and Understanding in a Transient World.

> *Obstinate and mindless*
> *Block of Stone,*
> *Lying here*
> *On this green moss,*
> *Oblivious of rain and dew,*
> *Immune to frost and snow.*
> *How many times has this garden*
> *Flourished and Decayed!*
> *How often have these flowers and trees*
> *Bloomed and Faded!*
> *Just ask old Mr. Stone—*
> *He remembers it all!*

WE DID IT OURSELVES!

The Highest Rulers
Were beyond Knowledge.
Those beneath them
Were loved and praised.
Those lower still were feared,
The lowest of all were reviled.
Wherever Trust
Is lacking on High,
It is lacking Below.
The Taoist is Distant,
Sparing with Words.
Whatever is Accomplished,
Whatever occurs,
The common folk declare:
"We did it of our own accord,
We did it ourselves!"

THE RIVER MASTER

The Highest were
True Gentlemen,
Supreme Rulers
Of Highest Antiquity.
They had No Name,
But an Abundance
Of Natural Simplicity.

Their subjects did not know of them directly, but sensed their existence somewhere High Above.

Beneath them
Were the Taoists,
Loved and praised
For Inner Power,
For True Benevolence.

Beneath these again were Rulers feared for devising harsh laws and punishments, reviled for issuing troublesome prohibitions and decrees. When an
inferior Ruler lacks Good Faith, subjects in their turn deceive their Ruler and
are devious. The Taoist Rulers of Antiquity were never far from the Tao.
Whenever something was Accomplished, there was Great Peace and Contentment throughout the land and the folk proclaimed: "We did it ourselves!"
They were oblivious of the Simple Strength of their Ruler's Inner Power.

MAGISTER LIU

"We did it of our own accord, we did it ourselves!" This is the Highest Tao,
the Tao of Non-Action, which casts its Net the widest. It cannot be seen, it
cannot be heard.

The Taoist
Is loath to speak
Of the Tao.

When a goal is Accomplished, the folk think that things have happened of their own accord. Taoists of Great Inner Power do not consider the Tao to be personal or private, they share it generously, they want everyone to Cultivate Life-Destiny. The folk think they have gained Possession of the Tao of Nature themselves, that they have "done it of their own accord."

Waley: It is by not believing Others, by not trusting them, that you turn them into liars. Similarly it is the "lack" of a quality in the Ruler which creates in the people every other fault and crime.

Duyvendak: The ideal relationship between Ruler and subject is that in which one is scarcely aware, or not aware at all, of the existence of the Ruler, who does everything through Non-Action.

Hanshan Deqing (1564–1623) describes the Serenity of a Zen Master, Zen being, as so often, close to the Tao.

> *Body like dead wood,*
> *Thoughts like ashes,*
> *Snow on my skull,*
> *Frost on my jaw.*
> *It's not that I disdain the world*
> *Because I am old.*
> *The Dust can find nowhere in my eyes*
> *To land.*

DECAY OF THE TAO

When the Great Tao Decays,
Benevolence and Righteousness
Come into Being.
When Intelligence and Wisdom
Come to the fore,
Great Hypocrisy
Arises.
When the Six Bonds are
Out of Kilter,
Filial Devotion and Compassion
Arise.
When the Nation is in Tumult,
Loyalty of the subject
Arises.

THE RIVER MASTER

When the Great Tao Prevails, Children feel a natural sense of Devotion to their Parents. Genuine Loyalty and Trust, True Benevolence and True Righteousness abound. When the Great Tao Decays, then Resentment and Rebellion Prevail, then False Benevolence and False Righteousness abound. Rulers of False Intelligence and Wisdom have no respect for Inner Power but set great store on Words, they think little of Substance and set great store on Appearance. Rulers such as these cause their Subjects to respond with Hypocrisy and Deceit. When the Tao Decays, when the Six Natural Bonds of Family are broken and the Six Natural Threads of Community are torn, then relatives and friends no longer live in Natural Harmony, then False Devotion and Insincere Compassion abound.

When the Great Tao
Prevails,
False Virtues
Disappear,
Like stars which fade
When the sun is fully risen.

MAGISTER LIU

The Great Tao Encompasses and Connects everything. If it Decays, then all so-called Virtues lose their Root. They have Name but no Substance. Instead there is Great Hypocrisy, there is Discord and Tumult. The Great Tao brings all together as One Whole. The Great Tao is the Original Mother of All. If the Mother once Decays, then these Virtues have no Root, they do not arise naturally, Of-Themselves. They are forced and hypocritical.

Hold the Tao
Close.
Do not let it
Decay.

Waley: The Six Bonds were those between father, son, elder brother, younger brother, husband, and wife.

Duyvendak: This Chapter is directed against the school of Confucius and its moral precepts, against its insistence on artificial obedience to the discipline of Rites and Moral Education. If all things are allowed to follow the course of the Tao of Nature, without human intervention or constraint, then there is no need of these so-called Virtues, which are contrary to human nature, and only exist as a reaction against a corrupt society. They are evidence of the Decay of the True Tao.

The poet Su Dongpo:

> *My white hairs wave*
> *In the frosty breeze.*
> *Here on this rattan cot*
> *In my small cottage*
> *I rest my ailing frame.*
> *A Taoist monk*
> *Sees me snoozing soundly*
> *On this Spring Day,*
> *And gently strikes*
> *The fifth watch bell.*

SIMPLE UNDYED SILK

Do away with Sages,
Discard Wisdom.
The folk will Benefit
A hundredfold.
Do away with Benevolence,
Discard Righteousness.
The folk will Return
To True Devotion
And Compassion.
Do away with Cunning,
Discard Profit,
And there will be no Thieves.
If these injunctions
Do not suffice,
Gaze upon
Simple Undyed Silk,
Embrace
The Uncarved Block,
Think less of Self,
Diminish Desire.

THE RIVER MASTER

To do away with the Meddling of the Sages brings a Return to the Beginning, to the Origin. The Five Emperors suspended the constellations in the Firmament, the Sage Cang Jie invented writing with ideograms. But superior to these was the Simplicity of the Three August Ones of Ancient Days, who communicated with Knotted Cords and dispensed with writing altogether.

> Return to
> Non-Action!
> Let the Tao
> And its Inner Power
> Of-Themselves
> Transform all
> So that it
> Returns
> To Simplicity.

Discard Cunning, do away with the Deceit which merely sows Chaos and Discord.

> Gaze upon
> Simplicity,
> Hold fast to
> Nature,
> To the So-of-Itself.

MAGISTER LIU

Diminish the Desire of Self, do away with False Wisdom and Artifice, safeguard the Substance of the Tao. Discard Cunning and Profit, and there will be an end to Plotting and Greed. Purity of Thought will fill the Heart-and-Mind of the folk. They will be content with their lot and will not steal. With due time and the burgeoning Breath-Energy of the Tao, True Wisdom will take the place of False Wisdom, True Kindness will take the place of False Benevolence.

Waley: Doing away with Cunning means doing away with skilful artisans and enterprising traders, who supply things that are likely to attract thieves. Simple Undyed Silk (*su*) is a symbol of the "attributeless" nature of the Tao. The Uncarved Block (*pu*) is a symbol of the primal undifferentiated unity underlying the apparent complexity of the universe.

Duyvendak: The Chapter speaks of a Return from the dead letter of moral precepts to a Taoist state of Simplicity (Undyed Silk, the Uncarved Block) without Culture or Artifice.

Tao Yuanming aspired to a Simple Taoist life.

> Ah, how short a time it is that we are here! Why do we not then set our hearts at rest, and cease to fret whether we remain or go? Why wear out the soul with anxious thoughts? I desire neither wealth nor rank: I have no hopes of Heaven. Let me stroll in my garden through the bright hours of morning, among my flowers, or let me mount the hill and sing a song, or weave my verses beside the limpid brook. Thus will I live out my allotted span, content with the appointments of Fate, my spirit free from care.

AN INFANT YET TO SMILE

Do away with Learning,
And there is an end to Sorrow.
"How different is Yes from No!
How Good differs from Bad!
What others fear must surely be feared."
Such propositions
Confuse,
And there is no end to them!
Others rejoice
As if at a Great Feast,
Gaily ascending a Terrace in Spring.
I alone am forlorn,
Giving no outward sign,
Like an Infant yet to smile.
I am listless,
As though I have no Home.

Others have a Superfluity,
I alone am lacking.
Mine is the Heart-and-Mind
Of the Pure Fool!
The Multitude are bright and lively,
I alone am dull;
The common folk are alert,
I alone am sluggish,
Restless as the ocean,
Drifting endlessly.
Others have Means,
A Purpose.
I alone am a dolt,
A pauper.
Unlike them,
I prize the Nourishment
Of the Mother.

THE RIVER MASTER

The Learned are insincere, they are not in tune with the Tao.

When the frippery
Of this Learning
Is stripped away,
There is an end to Sorrow.

Others are joyful and dissolute, driven by Emotion and Desire, greedily anticipating a Great Feast, dissatisfied with their lot.

I alone am
Forlorn and quiet,
With no sign
Of Emotion or Desire,

They climb a Terrace in Spring, and from the Terrace they gaze around them lasciviously, the sexual congress of Yin and Yang foremost in Heart-and-Mind.

I am like
An Infant
Not yet able
To smile,
Not yet ready
To take part
In the season of mating.
I am listless,
With no place to go,
A poor rustic
With no Home,
A derelict.

Mine is the Heart-and-Mind of a Fool. I am utterly ignorant! The Multitude are bright and penetrating, I alone am dull and wrapped in darkness.

I drift
Like the boundless floods
Of River and Ocean,
Seeking repose
In the Realm of Spirit.
Others have a Purpose,
I practice Non-Action.
I prize the Nourishment
Of the Mother,
The Tao.

MAGISTER LIU

Be rid of all Cleverness and False Knowledge, Return to Simplicity, to True Knowledge. Once Desire is quelled, once False Learning is done away with, Calamity can gain no foothold, and there is an end to sorrow.

I am homeless,
My Heart-and-Mind

Drifts in the Tao,
My one Home.
Others busily Contend,
Wasting Spirit.
Others sparkle and are bright,
I am dull and listless,
Like the boundless Ocean.

Waley: A child "gives a sign" [and smiles] by stretching its hand towards some object. This is an important Omen concerning its future. Nourishment is from the Mother's breast—i.e., from suckling the Tao. The image may equally be that of a child in the womb, "feeding [internally] on the Mother." "What others fear . . ."—this saying or proposition refers to the need to keep the same taboos, ritual avoidances, etc. as people with whom one finds oneself in contact. The Taoist, who is the antithesis of other men, cannot obey these conformist rules. Fear, pettiness, meanness—all those qualities that pollute the "temple of the mind"—are due to a shrinkage of the life-spirit. The Spring Terrace was originally the scene of a kind of carnival, a period of authorized license intended, as such festivals always are, to promote the fertility of the fields.

Duyvendak: The study of the formal rules of etiquette and correct behavior has no end. The Taoist behaves like a Divine Fool. I seem stupid and limited, others seem clever. I stay in the shadows, I do not parade my abilities, instead I meditate on [find Nourishment from] the Mother, the Tao. Some see this image of the Tao-Mother as a Mother-Goddess. The Taoists certainly elevated the feminine as symbol of the Tao, but they did not personify the Tao as a goddess.

Taoist Hermits living in obscurity, with "no place to go," like poor rustics with no Home, were a favorite subject for Chinese poets and artists through the ages, exemplars of the Natural Life. Sometimes they were to be encountered in the suburbs; more often they were sought out deep in the mountains.

Lu Ji (261–303), "Summoning a Hermit":

> To still the Unquiet Mind
> The Hermit dwells
> In a secluded valley,
> In the morning
> Gathers cress
> By the southern waterfall,
> In the evening
> Rests
> At the foot of the western hills . . .
> The plashing of the mountain stream,
> The cleansing jade-song of the cascade:
> Perfect Joys such as these,
> The unsullied Simplicity
> Of the Uncarved Block,
> Cannot be feigned.

GRAND POWER

Grand Power
Flows from the Tao.
The Substance of the Tao
Is Vague and Misty.
Misty and Vague,
But it contains Images!
Its Substance
Is Tenuous and Dark!
But it contains an Essence,
Supremely Real,
Sure and Unfailing.
From days of old
It has been present,
The Source of All Things.
How do I know the Source,
The Father?
Only through this,
Through the Tao.

THE RIVER MASTER

The Grand Power of the Tao is Misty, it has no fixed identity, but there is nonetheless a Substance deep within it, a One, which brings about the Changes in All-under-Heaven, which Nourishes Breath-Energy and establishes Reality. The Tao conceals its Worth, it hides its Glory. How do I know this? I know it through the authentic evidence of this present moment, in which I see all beings receive the Breath-Energy of the Tao, I see them live and thrive in the Tao.

MAGISTER LIU

The Grand Power is
Unseen,
Unheard.
The Power is the Tao,
The Tao is the Power.

To discard Learning is to Cultivate Inner Power. To be Nourished by the Mother is to follow the Tao. The Power never ceases to be Calm even in Motion, it never ceases to be One with the Tao.

The Grand Power
Of the Tao
Is Misty,
And yet somewhere
Deep in that Mist
There seem to be
Images,
A Substance.

These Images are No-Image. This Substance is composed of Inchoate Matter, it is No-Substance. They merge in the Misty, Tenuous Darkness of the One, of the Tao.

Waley: "Through this" means through inward Knowledge, through the intuition of the Tao.

Duyvendak: The Grand Power is a spiritual force, which pervades all things.

JM: The word *xin*, literally Trust, which I translate as Sure and Unfailing, has given rise to a bewildering host of interpretations, but common to most of them is the idea of an infallible, authentic, credible core of evidence (experience of the Truth, of the innermost Essence of the Tao and its Power). The nineteenth-century French sinologist Stanislaus Julien calls it *"témoignage infaillible"*—infallible evidence of the Spiritual Essence of the Tao. Here the late-nineteenth-century German-American monist Paul Carus bursts into rhyme:

> *It harbors the Spirit Pure,*
> *Whose truth is ever sure,*
> *Whose faith abides for aye,*
> *From yore until today.*

Wei Yingwu (737–ca. 792) sought an elusive Hermit, lost in the misty mountains of the Tao.

> *My office has grown cold today,*
> *And suddenly I think of my mountain friend,*
> *Gathering firewood*
> *Down in the valley,*
> *Returning Home*
> *To boil white stones . . .*
> *I'd like to take him*
> *A cup of wine,*
> *To cheer him*
> *Through the evening storm.*
> *But fallen leaves*
> *Have strewn his mountain wilderness,*
> *And I shall never find*
> *His tracks.*

EMBRACING THE ONE

The Curved is Whole,
The Twisted Straight.
The Hollow Full,
The Worn New.
The Poorly Endowed
Attain their goal,
The Greatly Endowed
Go astray.
The Taoist
Embraces the One,
A Model for All-under-Heaven,
Shines
But never displays,
Is Radiant
But never Proud.
Accomplishes
But never Boasts,
Endures
But never Brags.
With the Non-Contending of the Taoist,
All-under-Heaven
Cannot Contend.
The old saying

"The Curved is Whole"
Is no empty talk!
No,
The Curved
Finds its Way Home,
Is truly Whole.

THE RIVER MASTER

The Curved Flows
With All-under-Heaven,
And is Whole.
The Twisted makes Others
Straight,
And is Straight itself.
Earth's Hollows
Receive the Flow of Water.
The Humble are
Home for Inner Power,
Protected by the Tao
Of Heaven-and-Nature.
The Spirit of the Tao
Glows in Emptiness.
Whosoever Possesses
Overmuch
Is confounded.
Whosoever Studies
Overmuch
Doubts what has been learned.
Whatsoever is Curved,
Whatsoever Flows,
Returns Home
To the Father and the Mother,
Safe from Harm.

MAGISTER LIU

Whosoever Embraces the One
And never Contends,
Whosoever is Gently Curved
And Glows without displaying,
Whosoever is Radiant
Without affirming Self,
Whosoever Prevails
Without glorifying Self,
Without boasting,
Such a one
Is Truly Whole,
Finds the Way Home,
Endures.
This is to Embrace the One,
To be Woman, not Man,
To Resonate
With All-under-Heaven,
With Inner Power Whole.
The Taoist knows
The Usefulness of the Useless,
The Utility of Futility.
The Taoist Spirit
Embraces Life-Destiny,
Finds the Way Home,
Truly Whole.

The Book of Taoist Master Zhuang: All know the Usefulness of the Useful. They do not know the Usefulness of the Useless.

Waley: The Way Home is the way to the Tao (the Way).

Lin Yutang: Behind all the paradoxes in this Chapter is the philosophy of Eternal Cycles, of things reverting to their opposites: the utility of futility, preservation [Wholeness] through Yielding [being Curved], the virtue of Not-Contending.

Wilhelm: The Curved is the new Moon, which becomes full. The Twisted is a caterpillar or rope which changes from a state of tension to one of relaxation. The Empty is the hollow in the ground that fills with Water. The Worn is the self-renewing foliage of a tree.

JM: The aesthetic of the Curved which makes things Whole, finding its Way Home to the Tao, can be seen throughout the Chinese arts of calligraphy and painting, and in the curving or winding path so ubiquitous in Chinese garden design. This aesthetic also underlies the art of Chinese musical theater, in which the actors' movements are always sinuous and curved, like the Tao. Li Dou writes in his memoir, *The Pleasure Boats of Yangzhou* (1795): Every new twist and turn leads on to yet another splendor.

Lin (in *The Chinese Theory of Art*): In painting, the line should never look as if made with a ruler, which is dead because it is perfectly straight.

Wei Yingwu, like Tao Yuanming, yearned to build himself a cabin out of town, to Return, to find his Way Home, to escape from "the pavements gray," and find some Peace "in the deep heart's core."

> *Cramped yearlong*
> *In my office,*
> *I stroll out of town*
> *In the bright light of dawn,*
> *To where willows*
> *Blow with the wind,*
> *And green hills*
> *Still my cares.*
> *Leaning against a tree*
> *I take my rest,*
> *Then wander back and forth*
> *Along the stream.*

A spring dove
Calls from its hidden nest,
The fragrant meads
Are wet with mist.
This Quietude
Is so easily Perturbed,
The affairs of the World
Make it restless again.
One day I shall finally Retire
And build a cabin here,
As Tao Yuanming did long ago.

TO FLOW WITH THE TAO

The Tao of Nature
Is sparing with Words.
A whirlwind
Doesn't last all morning,
A cloudburst
Doesn't last all day.
If these Things of Heaven and Earth
Do not last,
What then of Man?
To Flow with the Tao
Is to be part of the Tao.
To possess Inner Power,
Is to be part of the Power.
To suffer Failure
Is to be part of Failure.
Those who are part of the Tao,
The Tao takes to itself gladly.
Those who are part of the Power,

The Power takes in gladly.
Those who are part of Failure,
Failure receives gladly.
Lack of Trust
Creates Lack of Trust.

THE RIVER MASTER

To be sparing with Words is the Way of Nature and the Tao. Those who Flow with the Tao are peaceful and quiet, they Eschew Impulse and Desire, they Eschew Words, all of which resemble the Violence of the whirlwind and the cloudburst.

MAGISTER LIU

The Tao has nothing to say. To utter Words is a form of purposeful Action. Like the whirlwind and the cloudburst, Words do not last. The Taoist utters Few Words and never engages in a deliberate quest for Inner Power, for the Tao. They come of their own accord. The Taoist's Heart-and-Mind Flows with the Tao, Trusts in the Tao utterly, is part of the Tao, part of the Power, Surrenders to Life-Destiny. Run-of-the-mill Teachers, like the whirlwind and the cloudburst, lack Trust, lack Faith, lack Endurance. They do not Surrender to the Tao, they turn their backs on Non-Action. Instead they seek out the strange, they hanker after the unusual, they engage restlessly in outlandish practices, they are in one place early in the morning, somewhere else in the evening. They wear themselves out, they grow old unfulfilled. How sad this is!

Duyvendak: Like short-lived natural explosions, Words are a form of Violence which does not Endure. Instead of striving to Achieve a goal, we should take things as they come, we should let them unfold. If we succeed, well and good. If we fail, that is good too. This is the Flow of the Tao. Compare *The Book of Taoist Master Zhuang*, Chapter 2: "Do not rejoice at Success, do not mourn Failure."

Waley: If one uses disbelief [Lack of Trust] as an instrument of government, the result will be a nation of liars.

Tao Yuanming surrendered to the Flow of the Tao.

> I busy myself in my garden hoeing, cultivating, planting, or tending. I rejoice in my books, and am soothed by the music of my Lute. In the winter I warm myself in the sun, in the summer I bathe in the brook. I have received little enough reward for my labor, but my mind has enjoyed a constant leisure. In this way, Content with Heaven and accepting my Lot, I have lived out the years of my life.

THE TAOIST REALM

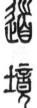

It's hard
To stand on tiptoe.
It's hard
To walk with legs akimbo.
Whosoever displays Self
Does not Truly Shine.
Whosoever vaunts Self
Is not Truly Radiant.
Whosoever boasts of Self
Does not Prevail.
Whosoever brags of Self
Does not Endure.
For the Taoist
These indulgences are like
Overeating,
Superfluous Action.
They are
To be Eschewed,
They are not the Taoist Realm.

THE RIVER MASTER

Whosoever chooses Force, whosoever loves Glory and strives for Fame, will never stand upright for long in the Tao. Whosoever glorifies Self and places Self above Others, whosoever straddles Others, will find the way ahead obstructed, will be unable to walk forward.

MAGISTER LIU

The Taoist Realm differs from the Realm without the Tao just as Soft and Gentle differ from Hard and Strong.

> To love
> Eminence and Fame
> Is like
> Standing on tiptoe.
> It cannot Endure,
> It will Fail.
> To love Force
> Is like
> Trying to walk with legs akimbo,
> With an exaggerated stride,
> Straining to outdo others
> In strength.
> It cannot Endure,
> It will end in Failure.

Love of Eminence and love of Force, the Heart-and-Mind of Victory, these know only Self, they do not know Others. They boast and brag, they cannot Glow with a True Light.

Waley: The Taoist does not linger at the scene of success, or call attention to it.

Duyvendak: All Excess is harmful. The Taoist is humble and discreet.

Liu Changqing (ca. 710–ca. 787), in his poem "Snowy Night on Lotus Mountain," evokes with a few deft strokes the Pure Taoist Realm.

Sunset.
Blue peaks
Fade into the distance.
Under a cold sky
A humble cabin
White with snow.
Dogs bark tonight
At the wicker gate.
Through the blizzard
Someone is coming home.

NATURE, THE SO-OF-ITSELF

There was a thing
Inchoate but Whole,
Before Heaven and Earth.
Silent!
Without Form!
Alone, unchanging,
Roaming far and wide,
Never Perishing,
Mother of All-under-Heaven.
I do not know
Its True Name,
I call it the Tao.
If I must use Words,
I call it Great,
It Passes On,
On into the Distance.
It is Distant,

And then Returns.
The Tao is Great,
Heaven is Great,
Earth is Great,
The King is Great.
In the Regions of the World
These are
The Four Great Things,
And the King of Men
Is one among them.
He models himself on Earth,
Earth on Heaven,
Heaven on the Tao,
The Tao models itself
On Nature,
On the So-of-Itself.

THE RIVER MASTER

The Tao is
Everywhere.
It is in Yang
But not Scorched by Yang.
It Yields to Yin
But does not Decay in Yin.
It threads all things
Together,
And is never
In Peril.

Man models himself on Earth, the Peaceful and Quiet, the Soft and Harmonious, the Provider.

Seeds sown
Within Earth
Bring forth
The Five Grains.
Deep beneath are
Sweet Springs.

Earth models itself on Heaven, the Still and Motionless, the Generous, giving without demanding any reward. Heaven models itself on the Tao, the Clear, the Calm and Silent. The Tao models itself on Nature, the So-of-Itself. The Tao *is* Nature. It has no other model.

MAGISTER LIU

The Tao is Nature. Nature is the Tao. All is Embraced and Threaded Together within the One, within the Tao. It is Ultimate Being within Ultimate Non-Being, Ultimate Substance within Ultimate Emptiness. The Tao contains all things in its Greatness. It is everywhere, it "passes on" from one place to another, through every Connected Place into the Distance. And from that Distance, it Turns, it begins again, it Returns. This Flow of Breath-Energy, this Cycle, is never broken, it has no End. Everything in All-under-Heaven is part of it, partakes of this Breath-Energy.

Waley: The Return is "to what was there at the Beginning," to the "unconditioned," the "what-is-so-of-itself." By passing on and on through successive stages of consciousness, back to the initial Unity, one can arrive at the Tao, which controls the multiform apparent Universe. As Taoist Master Zhuang wrote in his Chapter "Far Away Wandering," wanderings "alone with the Tao in the Great Wilderness" are not external journeys, but explorations of oneself, back to the "Beginning of Things."

This Return was very much on the mind of Tao Yuanming.

A dog barks
In the deep lanes,
A cock crows
Atop a mulberry tree.
No Dust and Confusion
Within door and courtyard.
In the empty rooms,
More than enough leisure.
I lived too long
Within a barred cage,
Now I can Return again
To Nature.

GRAVITY AND CALM

Gravity is the Root of Levity,
Of all that is Light.
Calm is Master of the Rash,
Of Impulse.
The Taoist when traveling
Never strays far
From the Baggage Cart,
Sees beyond the Finest Palace.
There is no remedy
For the Lord of a Myriad Chariots,
Who makes Light
Of All-under-Heaven.
Levity loses the Root.
Rashness forfeits the Mastery.

THE RIVER MASTER

A Ruler without Gravity is not respected. So too, when a Taoist practices Self-Cultivation without Gravity, Spirit is lost.

> Flowers and leaves
> Are Light.
> They Perish
> From their Levity.
> Roots are weighty,
> They last.
> Without Calm
> The Taoist invites Peril.
> Dragons are Calm,
> They Transform themselves
> At will.
> Tigers are Rash,
> They Die young.
> The Taoist,
> Walking all day in the Tao,
> Never strays far from
> The Baggage Cart
> Of Gravity and Calm.

A Light-minded and Rash Ruler, who wallows in luxury and frivolous sensuality, forfeits the respect of his Ministers. So too, flippant Practice of the Tao loses the Root.

MAGISTER LIU

In All-under-Heaven nothing is weightier, nothing has more Gravity, more Calm, than the Tao. The Taoist Eschews the Light and the Rash, Cleaves to the Weighty and the Calm, to Root and Master. Others treat Gravity with Levity, disturb Calm with Impulse, and in so doing lose Root and Master. Woe betide them!

The Taoist never strays far from the Baggage Cart of Gravity and Calm, never slackens, sees beyond the palaces and finery that delude Heart-and-Mind.

The Taoist's
Heart-and-Mind
Is a Bright Mirror.
It reflects
But does not absorb.
It is Still Water,
Calm without a ripple.

Waley: The Mastery is Calm, the magical passivity that is also called Non-Action (*wuwei*).

The Book of Master Lie (Lieh-tzu) is a later Taoist Classic which combines High Seriousness and Wise Wit—not to be confused with inappropriate Levity. In the following dialogue, Self-Cultivation, the Attainment of the Tao, is seen as a Not-Possessing, attained with Calm and a sense of No-Self.

The Legendary Emperor Shun asked one of his Ministers: "Can one Possess the Tao?"

"Your own body is not your Possession. How can you Possess the Tao?"

"If my own body is not mine, whose is it?"

"It is the Form lent you by Heaven and Earth. Your Life is not your Possession. It is a Harmony granted you for a time by Heaven and Earth. Your Life-Destiny is not your Possession. It is a Flow granted you for a time by Heaven and Earth. Your children and grandchildren are not your Possessions. Heaven and Earth have lent them to you to be cast off as an insect sheds its skin. You are the Breath-Energy of Heaven and Earth. How can you ever Possess that?"

LINEAGE OF LIGHT

The best Traveler
Leaves no Tracks,
The best Words
Contain no Flaws.
The best Counting
Uses no Abacus.
The best Door
Has neither Bolt nor Key,
But cannot be opened.
The best Knot
Is not Tied,
But can never be loosened.
The True Taoist saves Others,
Rejects no one,
Saves things,
Rejects nothing.
In the Lineage of Light,
The Best Teach the Not-so-Good,
The Not-so-Good are Material
To be taught by the Best.
Despite any amount of acquired Knowledge,
Not to Esteem
One's Teacher,

Not to Cherish
One's Material,
Is to be greatly lost.
This is the Lineage of Light,
A Most Marvelous Mystery.

THE RIVER MASTER

The best Traveler
Walks in the Tao,
Leaves no Tracks,
Travels within Self,
Enters no Hall,
Passes through no Gate.

The best Words contain no lingering trace of Flawed Judgment. The Taoist, who Embraces the One, the Tao, has no need of Abacus in order to count. The Door of the Tao is closed through Cessation of Desire, through Retention of Essence, without need of Bolt or Key. The Knot tied within the Heart-and-Mind of the Tao can never be untied. The Taoist is free of Judgment, does not hold the commonest stone in low regard, does not prize the most precious jade. The True Lineage of Light is a Transmission from Teacher to Disciple. If the Disciple does not Esteem the Teacher, if the Teacher does not deign to Teach, then the Transmission is broken. Without this Lineage of Light, however hugely knowledgeable and clever and wise one may think oneself to be, one loses the way. To fathom this is to fathom a Great Mystery of the Tao.

MAGISTER LIU

To Know that, despite any amount of Knowledge, one has lost one's way is a Higher Knowledge. Deep within this sense of being lost is a Knowledge that is No-Knowledge. Its Transmission is the True Lineage of Light, which is One with Nature, with the So-of-Itself. This is a Great Mystery.

Rémi Mathieu: The Lineage (*ximing*) is the Illumination of the Tao Transmitted by the Taoist Perfecti to Others.

Waley: The Light has been defined as Self-Knowledge. This Light is how the Taoist saves the world, though apparently shunning it. The Most Marvelous Mystery, the Lineage, Transmits the Power to influence mankind through the Tao. The commonest charge brought against Taoists was that of being merely interested in Self-Perfection without regard for the welfare of the community as a whole. The present Chapter is devoted to rebutting that charge.

JM: Retention of Essence, in the River Master's Commentary, is almost certainly an early reference to the Taoist Sexual Practice of seminal retention, what Joseph Needham calls *coitus thesauratus*, whereby the man refrains from ejaculation, and causes his sperm (Essence) to "return" and nourish the brain. (*Science and Civilisation in China*, vol. 2, pp. 145–153.)

The Book of the Prince of Huainan is a lengthy early compendium containing Taoist Teachings and numerous quotations from *The Tao and the Power*. It, like so many other Taoist Classics, and their Commentaries, Transmits the Lineage of the Perfecti. Here is a typical passage from a section entitled "The Nature of the Tao":

> The Tao Roofs over Heaven. It is the Foundation of the Earth. It extends North, South, East, and West, stretching to the Eight Extremities in all directions. Its Height is beyond reach, its Depth unfathomable. It enfolds both Heaven and Earth, and gives Birth to things which were without Form. Like a Spring, it bubbles up from nothing but gradually forms a volume of rushing muddy water, which then gradually settles and becomes clear. It is inexhaustible, knowing neither the Plenitude of Morning nor the Decay of Night. When dispersed, it is vast as space. When compressed, it is barely a handful. It is both Scant and Ample, both Dark and Bright. It is both Weak and Strong, both Soft and Hard. It is open on all sides, but contains within itself the Yin and the Yang. It binds up the Universe, and makes manifest the sun, moon, and stars. It is dense as Clay, and

yet thin as Water. It is infinitesimally fine, and yet can still be divided. It makes the mountains to rise high, and the valleys to sink low. It makes beasts to walk, birds to fly, the sun and moon to shine, the stars to move, the unicorn to come forth, and the phoenix to hover above us.

THE UNCARVED BLOCK

Know Man,
Cleave to Woman.
Be a Ravine
For All-under-Heaven,
With Constant Power
That never fades.
Return Home
To the Infant.
Know the White,
Cleave to the Black.
Be a Model
For All-under-Heaven,
With Constant Power
That never fails.
Return Home
To the Infinite.
Know Honor,
Cleave to No-Honor.
Be a Valley
For All-under-Heaven,
With Constant Power
That suffices.
Return Home
To the Uncarved Block.

When the Block is split
It forms utensils,
Which can be used
By the Taoist
As Chief Officer.
The Greatest Carver
Does the least cutting.

THE RIVER MASTER

Put aside Man,
Hard and Strong,
Cleave to Woman,
Soft and Gentle.

Be Humble and Lowly, like a Deep Ravine, and the Power is Constant. All-under-Heaven Comes Home to the One, like Water pouring into a Deep Ravine. Return Home to the Infant, to Folly, to No-Knowledge. White is Luminous. Black is Silent. The Illuminated remain Silent and Dark. The Taoist practices Self-Cultivation, stills Desire through the Great Tao, keeps Spirit Whole and safe from Harm.

MAGISTER LIU

Constant Power leads to Great Completion, the Completion of No-Cutting.

This is to Return Home
To the Uncarved Block,
To the Inchoate Fog,
To the Infant.
This is to put aside
Human Heart-and-Mind,
To Attain

The Heart-and-Mind
Of the Tao,
The Uncarved Block,
Which Transforms
Heart-and-Mind.

Self-Cultivation Returns first to the Infant, then to the Infinite, finally to the Uncarved Block, the True Elixir itself. The Taoist is now whole. This is to be a Valley, a Ravine, to be One with Emptiness, with Non-Action.

Waley: The Greatest Ruler does the least chopping about.

Wilhelm: The Infinite is the state before the Primal Beginning (*taiji*) in which all opposites are intermingled.

Duyvendak: True virility (Man) does not assert itself in Action but is passive, it Achieves all by Non-Action. Its Power collects like Water in a Ravine that never seeps away. Whosoever keeps to what is black, dark, Yin, in contrast to what is bright, white, Yang, is passive, like the one who Cleaves to Woman. For the Taoist, these contrasts are not real, they are only phases in the development of things.

In the words of Tao Yuanming again:

Let Go,
Float
On the Great Flux of things.

VESSEL OF SPIRIT

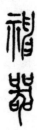

The Desire to Control
All-under-Heaven
Through Action
Cannot succeed.
All-under-Heaven
Is a Vessel of Spirit
That cannot be Ruled
Through Action,
That cannot be Controlled.
Acting upon it
Causes it to fail,
Controlling it
Spoils it.
Some walk ahead,
Some follow,
Some breathe in,
Some breathe out,
Some are strong,
Some are defeated,
Some nurture,
Some destroy.

The Taoist avoids Extremes,
Eschews Extravagance,
Eschews Grandeur.

THE RIVER MASTER

Rule through Action loses the True Tao of Heaven-and-Nature, it fails to win the Heart-and-Mind of the folk.

The vast Spirit Vessel of the World,
Of All-under-Heaven,
Loves Peace and Calm
Above all.
It cannot be Ruled
Through Action.
Meddling ruins it.
Ruling through Action
Violates
Its True Nature.

To impose Dogma on All-under-Heaven injures its True Essence, creates Hypocrisy and Deceit. By Eschewing Extravagance and Grandeur, by walking Simply and Harmoniously within Emptiness, in Moderation, in Non-Action, the Taoist causes All-under-Heaven to Transform itself Of-Itself.

MAGISTER LIU

The Vessel of Spirit cannot be Ruled through Action, it is Born of the Tao of Nature, the So-of-Itself. The slightest Action, the slightest attempt to Control it, violates its True Nature. All Action strays from the Tao of Nature. Spirit can only be Transformed through Inner Power, not through Action. The Uncarved Block, the Intact, the Unhewn, cannot be Ruled through Action. If the Uncarved Block is split and divided into utensils, then the Taoist, as Chief Officer Ruling All-under-Heaven, may perhaps resort to temporary Action in the World, but this is Action of Spirit, which is Non-Action. Worldly Leaders stride ahead and give orders to their followers, they Rule through Action. The Tao follows Nature and Innermost Substance. It never goes against the grain of things. If I Teach Others according to their own Nature and Innermost Substance, they happily accept me and my Teachings. This happens Of-Itself.

Only the Taoist,
Nourished
By the Primal Mother,
Can Rule
The Vessel of Spirit
In this way.

Wilhelm: The Vessel of Spirit is a spiritual organism which cannot be dealt with by contrived, soulless, or mechanical action.

Duyvendak: The general idea is clear. By forcing things one goes counter to their natural development, and consequently loses them. The Vessel of Spirit is probably an allusion to the Nine Sacred Bronze Vessels, which were symbolic of the Royal Power over the Nine Directions of All-under-Heaven, the "Empire."

The Spirit of Gentle and Harmonious Calm is well expressed by Qian Qi (722–ca. 780), awaiting the arrival of his friend.

At this little grass-hut in the valley,
As the evening clouds rise
Above the vine-clad wall,
The bamboos are fresh with rain,
The mountains tender in the sunset.
Cranes glide early to rest,
Autumn flowers slowly fade . . .
I bid my boy sweep the grassy path
For the coming of my friend.

AGAINST FORCE

A Ruler
Nourished by the Tao
Never takes up Arms,
Does no Violence
To All-under-Heaven.
In the wake
Of any military campaign
Violence rebounds,
Thorns and brambles
Spring up.
The passage of an Army
Is attended
With poor harvests.
The best general
Achieves his Goal
And Lets Go,
Never ventures
To take more by Force.
He Accomplishes
Without boasting,
Without bragging,

Without pride.

He Accomplishes

And Lets Go,

He stops short

Of Violence.

Brute strength

Decays with Age.

It is not the Tao.

Whatsoever is not the Tao

Meets with an early end.

THE RIVER MASTER

A Ruler Nourished by the Tao follows Heaven-and-Nature, uses Inner Power. The enemy Surrenders of its own accord. In times of War agriculture is neglected, fields are left uncultivated, crops are spoiled, harvests are poor. The Taoist Withdraws, Halts Military Action as soon as the Goal has been Accomplished. The Taoist never thinks of War as something fine, does not seek Fame by resorting to Violence, is resolute but not boastful, humble not proud.

MAGISTER LIU

The best general, Achieving his Goal and Letting Go, is both Hard and Soft, does not strive to Prevail by Force, is not tempted to conquer All-under-Heaven by Force of Arms.

The wiles

Of the Human Heart-and-Mind

Are brambles and thorns,

A poor harvest,

Futile expense of Spirit.

The Taoist Returns Home

To Nature,
To the So-of-Itself,
And thereby keeps Heart-and-Mind
Safe from Harm.
Brambles are Transformed
Into Healing Herbs,
The poor harvest
Becomes an Abundance.

Waley: *The Tao and the Power* devotes several Chapters (this one, 31, 68, and 69) to the condemnation of War . . . He who overcomes by Violence will be overcome by Violence. The "poor harvest" refers not only to direct destruction, but also to the curse that War brings upon herds and crops by its intrinsic "balefulness."

The harmful effects of Force and of Protracted War are a central concern of the strategic treatise attributed to Sun-tzu, *The Art of War*, which probably dates from about the same period as *The Tao and the Power*.

> Chapter 2: Without a full understanding of the Harm caused by War, it is impossible to understand the most profitable way of conducting it . . .

Like those early Chinese fascists, the Legalist thinkers (*fajia*) such as Master Hanfei, *The Art of War* often borrows Taoist ideas for its own purpose. It emphasizes, for example, the desirability of winning the upper hand without engaging in battle or using Force (the Warfare of the Heart-and-Mind).

> Chapter 3: Ultimate Excellence lies not in winning every battle but in defeating the enemy without ever fighting. The highest form of warfare is to attack Strategy itself . . . Know the enemy, know yourself, and Victory is never in doubt.

INSTRUMENTS OF ILL OMEN

Even the finest Weapons
Are Instruments of Ill Omen,
To be hated by all.
The Taoist
Does not Avail himself of them.
In his Dwelling
The True Gentleman
Esteems the Left,
In Warfare
He esteems the Right.
Weapons are not used
By the True Gentleman,
Except as a last resort.
Peace and Calm
Are always preferred.
Even in Victory
Weapons are not
Things of Beauty.

To think them beautiful
Is to rejoice in killing.
Joy in killing
Forfeits the allegiance
Of All-under-Heaven.
On Auspicious Occasions
The Left is prized,
For Inauspicious Affairs,
The Right.
The junior commander
Takes his stand
On the Left,
The senior commander
On the Right.
In Warfare,
When many lives have been taken,
Victory should be marked
With Rites of Mourning
And Lamentation.

THE RIVER MASTER

Weapons
Perturb Spirit,
They are
Instruments of Evil,
Never to be cultivated,
Never to be beautified.

The True Gentleman despises them. As a last resort they may occasionally be used, in times of chaos, when catastrophe looms. But Rulers bent on controlling the Destiny of Others with Force, with cruel punishments, lack the Tao and the Inner Power wherewith to Transform Others. They merely Harm the Innocent. In Ancient Times, the victorious general adopted the Rites of Mourning, wore white robes, and lamented.

MAGISTER LIU

By Weapons is meant any form of Violence that causes Harm. Violence is in itself an Instrument of Ill Omen and should never be employed except as a last resort. There is no intrinsic beauty in Victory. Force should be exercised as little as possible, with Moderation, never to Excess. Achieve a goal and Let Go. When Hard and Soft exist together in human affairs, this is the True Tao. The Taoist at Peace with Self is like a Nation in which even the finest weapons are not employed.

> Freed
> From the trammels
> Of Desire,
> The Taoist
> Cleaves to the One,
> Returns Home
> To the Real,
> To the Wondrous Realm
> Of Nature,
> To the So-of-Itself,
> To Non-Action,
> Soft within Hard,
> Hard within Soft.

Chen Guying: In Antiquity the Left was usually thought of as Yang and Auspicious, the Right as Yin, or Inauspicious. The True Gentleman Esteems the Right in Warfare, which is perverse and Inauspicious, and contrary to tradition.

Once more, compare Sun-tzu's *Art of War*, Chapter 1, Commentary by Li Quan (eighth century): "War is an Instrument of Ill Omen. It brings Life and Death, Survival and Extinction. A grave endeavor indeed, and one that men, alas, undertake too lightly."

And compare also Sun Bin's *Art of War*, Chapter 2: "War must be pondered carefully. The man who takes pleasure in War will perish. He who Benefits from War incurs dishonor. War is not a thing to be enjoyed. Victory is not something to Benefit from."

STREAMS AND VALLEYS

The Tao
Has no Name,
The Uncarved Block
Is Small,
But subject to None
In All-under-Heaven.
When Nobles and Kings
Cleave to it,
The Myriad Things
Willingly pay them homage.
Heaven and Earth as One
Send Sweet Dew,
The folk dwell
In Harmony
With no need of Decree.

Once the Uncarved Block
Is split apart,
Once there are Names,
Then know where to Halt,
Keep safe from Harm.
The Tao is
To All-under-Heaven
As the Great River
And the Ocean are
To Streams and Valleys.

THE RIVER MASTER

The Tao,
Like the Uncarved Block,
Is Simple.
It is Small,
And yet
Subject to nothing.

All-under-Heaven models itself on the Tao and Flows with Inner Power.
Heaven-and-Nature Resonate, bringing the Breath-Energy of Spirit, Sweet
Dew, to succor the folk, to keep them safe from Peril.

Spirit Resonates
In Harmony,
Flows
In abundance,
Like Streams and Valleys
Into the River and the Ocean.

MAGISTER LIU

The Uncarved Block is the Tao. It may be Small, but in its Simplicity and Power to command allegiance, to keep Others from Harm, it is Vast.

The Tao is present
In every single thing,
In each and every
Principle of things,
Just as every Stream and Valley
Flows down
To the Great River and the Ocean,
Just as the Myriad Things
Return Home
To their Root.
The Uncarved Block
Is an Emblem of the Tao,
It is Ruler of Nothing,
It seems so Small,
It abides in Non-Action.
To come to Rest
In the Uncarved Block,
To abide in it,
Is to be close
To the Tao,
And safe from Harm.
It is to live
In Simple Quietude and Calm.
The Myriad Modes of Being
Share a Single Root,
Like the many Streams and Valleys
Which Return Home
To the Great River and the Ocean,
Like the thousands of Threads,
The Myriad Strands,
Which are One Tao,
One Uncarved Block.

Waley: Sweet Dew tastes like barley-sugar or honey; it falls only when a king-dom is at complete peace. *Lun Heng* XIX, 2. Names are categories, distinctions. Such things depend on contrast with something else, as opposed to the Tao, which is So-of-itself.

Chen: The Sweet Dew is the Rain which Nourishes all Life.

Duyvendak: The Tao is the supreme example of Knowing where to Halt. It is like the streams which all flow to the lowest place, to the Great River and the Ocean.

Chan: Names break up original Simplicity and Unity, the Uncarved Block, and give rise to intellectual cunning and social discrimination. The Taoist must handle Names carefully, use them sparingly, never let them destroy the Unity of the Tao.

In the domain of Chinese painting, Taoist ideas prevailed. Painterly inspira-tion came from a state of Oneness with Nature, from the absence of Rules (or Names), from Harmony with the So-of-Itself, with the Uncarved Block. The painter Shitao (1642–1707) wrote in his *Propositions on Painting of the Bitter-Gourd Monk*:

> *In highest Antiquity*
> *There were no Rules.*
> *The Uncarved Block*
> *Had not yet been divided.*
> *When the Uncarved Block was divided,*
> *Rules came into being.*

KNOWING SELF

To understand Others
Is Wisdom,
To know Self
Is Illumination.
To vanquish Others
Requires Force,
To vanquish Self
Requires Strength.
To know Contentment
Is True Wealth.
To Persevere
Requires Will.
Not to lose one's Place
Is to Endure,
To Die but not to Perish,
Is Long Life.

THE RIVER MASTER

Whosoever Understands
The Likes and Dislikes
Of Others
Is Wise.
Whosoever Understands
The Strengths and Weaknesses
Of Self,
Whosoever hears
The Silence within,
Whosoever sees the Invisible,
Is Illumined.
Whosoever vanquishes
The Passion and Desire
Of Self
Prevails
In All-under-Heaven.

MAGISTER LIU

One's Place is where one should come to Rest, it is Home, the Tao. This is True
Knowledge. To pass Judgment on Others, to make distinctions between High
and Low, may seem like Knowledge, but is not.

To Know Self,
To wear sackcloth
And have Jade
In one's bosom,
Is to have True Knowledge
Within.
To Contend
Is not True Strength.
To vanquish Self,
To be Soft and not Forward,

May seem like
Weakness,
But is Strength
Within Self,
It is the True Judgment
That Eschews Force,
That abides in the Light,
In True Illumination.
It is an Abundance,
A Wealth that is
Never Full
To the Brim.

This is to Return Home to the Uncarved Block, to Purity, to Non-Action. This
is to Return to the Tao, to Knowledge of Self, where Being and Non-Being are
One, where Outer Radiance and Inner Marvel merge.

Waley: Longevity [Long Life] means, strictly speaking, potential longevity,
"staying-power," what we would call having a good constitution, and is a
quality that may be possessed by the young as well as the old. One branch of
the "life-nurturing" school of Taoism sought it by means of diet, hygiene,
drugs, etc.

Duyvendak: Not to lose one's Place means to accept one's Lot, not to force
anything by Excessive Action, not to try to reach full development before its
due time.

One of the famous Taoist Immortals, a Master of the techniques of Longevity,
was the legendary Sun Deng.

> Sun Deng was homeless. He lived in the mountains to the north
> of the district of Gong, in an underground cavern that he had made
> for himself. In summer he wove grasses to wear as a shirt and in
> winter he let his hair down to cover himself. He liked to read the *I
> Ching* and played a Lute with a single string. All who saw him were

well disposed toward him and took pleasure in his company. There was not an ounce of hatred or anger in him. He was once thrown into the water in an attempt to make him angry, but he just emerged from the water and broke into an enormous guffaw. From time to time he would wander among men and some of the householders he passed would set out food and clothing for him, none of which he kept. When he had taken his leave of them he just threw it all away. Once when he went to the Yiyang mountains he was seen by some charcoal-burners who could tell he was no ordinary man. But when they talked to him he did not answer.

This Sun was probably the same Immortal sought out by more than one of the Seven Sages of the Bamboo Grove. Ruan Ji ended up communicating with him in the time-honored Taoist mode of psychic "whistling."

Ruan Ji spied him squatting with clasped knees by the edge of a cliff. He climbed the ridge to approach him and squatted down opposite him. Ruan spoke to him briefly concerning matters from Antiquity to the Present, beginning with the Tao of Mystical Quietude of the Yellow Emperor and Shen Nong, and ending with an investigation of the excellence of the Supreme Inner Power of the Three Ages. But when Ruan asked for his views concerning these things Sun was aloof and said nothing. Ruan then went on to expound that which lies beyond Action, and the techniques of Calming the Spirit and Guiding the Breath-Energy. But when he looked to Sun for a reply, Sun remained exactly as before, fixedly staring straight ahead. Ruan then turned toward him and made a long whistling sound. After a long while the man finally laughed and said, "Do that again." Ruan whistled a second time, but by now he was beginning to lose interest, and he took his leave. He was about halfway down the ridge when he heard above him a great burst of music like the sound of an orchestra of many instruments. Again and again the forests and valleys echoed with the sound. Turning back to look, he saw that it was the whistling of the man he had just visited.

THE FLOOD

The Great Tao
Is a Flood,
Stretching left and right.
The Myriad Things
Cleave to it
And are Born.
It denies them nothing.
It Accomplishes
Without Naming.
It clothes and Nourishes
The Myriad Things
Without lording it over them.
It is free from Desire.
It takes the humblest of Names.
The Myriad Things
Return to it,
But owe it no allegiance.
By not Lording it over them
It can be called
Truly Great.

In not considering itself Great,
It Achieves
True Greatness.

THE RIVER MASTER

The Flood of the Tao
Floats,
It sinks,
It is,
It is not.
It cannot be seen,
It can hardly be described.
It is
Left and right.
It is
Everywhere.
The Tao
Rejects nothing.

MAGISTER LIU

The Tao is free of Desire, is humble, it never Lords it over Others. This is its Greatness.

The Flood
Of the Tao
Is like water
Blown by the wind,
Like waves rippling
To left and right,
Coming forth
And disappearing
In unfathomable ways.

The Myriad Things Cleave to it and are Born. The Myriad Things are Born from their Root in the Tao, they Flow with the Tao, they Return Home. Not one of them is ever lost, not one is ever abandoned. This is True Greatness. This is the Flood of the Tao. This is its Nature. Only one who Embraces the Tao can be both Great and Small, can Return Home.

Lin Yutang quotes Taoist Master Zhuang on the Omnipresence of the Tao. *The Book of Taoist Master Zhuang*, Chapter 22:

> The Master of East Wall asked Master Zhuang: "This thing called the Tao, wherein does it exist?" Master Zhuang replied: "It is every-where." "Please be more exact." "It is in an ant." "As low as that?" "It is in the smallest weed." "Lower still!" "It is in the tiniest shard." "How can it be so low?" "It is in piss and shit." The Master of East Wall fell silent.

Self-Cultivation, which is Embracing the Tao, the "formation" (in the French sense) of the Taoist Heart-and-Mind, lay at the root of all the pursuits of the Chinese *literatus*, the scholar-poet-artist. In the Chinese tradition, fine literature, fine art, fine calligraphy, and fine music were all of them manifestations of the Tao. The Chinese written language itself (*wen*), with its ancient and mysterious origins in the mythical Plan of the Yellow River and Scroll of the River Luo, was revered as a natural, organic expression of the Tao. The Chinese poet was descended from the ancient shamans, and acted as a medium for the Tao. Lu Ji (261–303), in his "Rhapsody on Literature," wrote:

> *Taking his position*
> *At the hub of things,*
> *The writer*
> *Contemplates*
> *The Dark Mystery of the universe . . .*
> *Gazing*
> *At the Myriad Things,*
> *He thinks of the richness*

Of the world.
At first he withholds sight,
And turns hearing inward . . .

The modern scholar Miao Yue (1904–1995) has written in a similar vein of the poet's high calling and Self-Cultivation, referring to the traditional genre of poetry known as lyric verse (*ci*):

> To those born with a sensitive spirit and an appreciation of subtle beauty, lyric verse can bring delight and release, it can be a source of peace. And this aesthetic sensitivity, if coupled with a sincere Self-Cultivation, can greatly enhance the quality of a man's everyday life and of his literary and scholarly pursuits. Many human activities coexist, many paths lead to the same goal. Lyric verse, an expression of the human Heart-and-Mind, and of human perceptions of the world, is one path leading to an understanding of beauty and goodness.

THE GREAT IMAGE

Cleave to
The Great Image,
And All-under-Heaven
Draws nigh,
Safe from Harm,
In Peace and Prosperity.
Music and fine food
Entice the Passerby to halt.
Words issuing from the Tao
Are bland,
They lack flavor.
Look at the Tao,
There is little to see,
Listen to it,
There is little to hear;
But Practice it,
And it is Infinite.

THE RIVER MASTER

The Great Image is the Tao. With Self-Cultivation, Heaven-and-Nature cause Spirit to descend and Commune with the Taoist. All-under-Heaven is at Peace.

> Wheresoever Joy or Beauty
> Is to be found,
> The Passerby
> Lingers,
> Abandons Plenitude
> To abide instead
> In Emptiness.

MAGISTER LIU

The Great Image is the Tao. The Tao has no flavor, it can be neither seen nor heard, and yet whosoever practices it is Nourished by the Primal Source, which is inexhaustible, which is Infinite. Whosoever Cleaves to the Tao can be both Small and Great.

> In its Origin
> The Tao is
> Calm and Flowing,
> In tune with Change.
> To Attain the Tao
> Is to dwell
> In Non-Action,
> To live
> In No-Business,
> To enter the Realm
> Of Silence,
> The finest Music,
> To sample
> The choicest delicacies,
> Like a lingering Passerby,

It is to unbind
The bindings
Of Heart-and-Mind,
To Flow
With Pure Resonance.

The Great Image is in Truth No-Image, the Cleaving is a Cleaving that is No-Cleaving, it is Ineffable.

In Words
The Tao is bland
And without flavor,
And yet it has the finest fragrance,
A Flavor
That is No-Flavor,
The Greatest
Of all Flavors.

Wang Bi: Music and fine food detain Passersby. But the words of the Tao are bland.

Duyvendak: Compare *The Book of Taoist Master Zhuang*, Chapter 22 (Legge's translation):
We look for it and there is no form; we hearken and there is no sound . . . The Tao cannot be heard; what can be heard is not it. The Tao cannot be seen; what can be seen is not it. The Tao cannot be expressed in Words; what can be expressed in Words is not it.

In Tao Yuanming's famous prose miniature, the Calm and Peaceful Ease of the Tao pervades the utopian community of Peach Blossom Spring. A fisherman stumbles upon an isolated valley, cut off from the march of time, living in happy Simplicity.

He found a small opening in the mountain, and light seemed to
be pouring through it. He left his boat and entered a cave, which at

first was extremely narrow, barely admitting his body. After a few dozen steps, it suddenly opened out onto a broad and level plain. There were well-built houses surrounded by paddy-fields and pretty ponds. Mulberry, bamboos, and other trees and plants grew there, and crisscross paths dotted the fields. The sounds of cocks crowing and dogs barking could be heard from one courtyard to the next. In the fields men and women came and went about their work. Old men and boys were all of them carefree and happy.

THE SUBTLE LIGHT

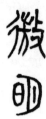

To Shrink,
First stretch.
To be Soft,
First be strong.
To destroy,
First raise up.
To steal,
First give away.
This is the Subtle Light.
Soft and Gentle
Prevail over
Hard and Strong.
Never take a fish
From its deep,
Never display
The Sharp Weapons
Of a Nation.

THE RIVER MASTER

Through the efficacy
Of the Subtle Light,
Soft and Gentle
Endure,
Hard and Strong
Perish.
Fish taken from the Deep
Cease to be Soft,
Cannot Return.

MAGISTER LIU

The Subtle Light
Is invisible,
Unknowable,
A fish
Lurking in the Deep,
A Weapon
Not shown to Others.

Cleaving to the Great Image, keeping All-under-Heaven safe from Harm,
Practicing the Tao, the Taoist holds the Handle with which to turn the Wheel
of Breath-Energy, of *Qian* and *Kun*, the first two Hexagrams of the *I Ching*.

Twin Principles,
Yang and Yin,
Creative and Receptive,
Action and Non-Action.

Those who Cleave to the Great Image will Master the Art of Life.

Wherein lies this Art?
It lies

In going with the Flow,
Guiding the Flow gradually
Till it Halts.
The Subtle Light
Lies hidden
Within,
Like a fish
In the Deep.
It glows,
Safe from Harm.
Fish find Nourishment
In the Deep.
If they are taken thence,
They Die.
The Taoist
Guided by the Subtle Light,
Is sheltered
From raging flames,
Tows a boat
Through muddy waters,
Unaffected
By the world.

Waley: The Taoist must be Small in order to be Great, must be cast down to be exalted, must remain like the fish at the bottom of the pool.

The *I Ching*, the Great Treatise: The Tao of *Qian* forms Man, the Tao of *Kun* forms Woman. *Qian* masters the Great Beginning . . . *Qian* and *Kun* are the Doors of Change. Closing the Door is *Kun*, opening the Door is *Qian*.

The Subtle Light of the Taoist incognito is well evoked in the words of Taoist Master Zhuang:

Do not be an embodier of Fame. Do not be a storehouse of schemes.
Do not be an undertaker of projects. Embody to the fullest that which

has no end, and wander where there is no trail. Hold on to all that you have received from Heaven, but do not think you Possess anything. Be Empty, that is all. The Perfectus uses Heart-and-Mind like a Mirror—going after nothing, welcoming nothing, responding but not storing. In so doing he Prevails and is safe from Harm.

TRANSFORMED

The Tao
Is True Non-Action,
Whereby all is
Accomplished.
When Nobles and Kings
Cleave to the Tao,
The Myriad Things
Are Transformed
Of their own accord.
But if they still
Crave Action,
I strengthen them
With the Nameless,
With the Uncarved Block,
With No-Desire,
With Calm.
Then All-under-Heaven
Settles of its own accord.

THE RIVER MASTER

If the Myriad Things are still subject to Desire, if they exhibit Cunning and Hypocrisy, the Ruler must strengthen them in their Aspirations, must buttress them by means of the Tao and the Power. Then they will be freed of Desire, and will be utterly Transformed through Clarity and Calm.

MAGISTER LIU

Non-Action,
Whereby
All is Accomplished,
Is a Transformation
That takes place
Of-Itself.
The folk Return
To the Uncarved Block
Of their own accord,
And all is Calm.
The Hundred Troubles
Are Transformed,
They Return
To Non-Being.
This is the kindling
Of the Subtle Light
Of the Tao,
No-Thought,
Non-Action.
True Calm.

The Tao is the Heart-and-Mind, the Heart-and-Mind is the Tao. All is Calm and Still, Resonant, Connected with Heaven and Earth.

Chen: To be Transformed is to be Born, to Flow and to reach Completion. When the Ruler Practices Non-Action, all things can develop according to their natural potential, expressing themselves freely and nurturing their own uniqueness. They have a stable and harmonious environment in which to grow.

In the Rhapsody "The Bones of Master Zhuang" by the astronomer-poet Zhang Heng (78–139), the deceased Taoist Master (or rather, his skeleton speaking from the roadside dust) evokes the Supreme Calm to be found in the Ultimate Transformation of Death.

> *In Death I rest and am at peace;*
> *In life I toiled and strove.*
> *Is the hardness of the winter stream*
> *Better than the melting of spring?*
> *All pride that the body knew,*
> *Was it not lighter than Dust?*
> *Death has hidden me*
> *In the Eternal Tao,*
> *Where neither leopard nor tiger can harm me,*
> *Lance prick me nor sword wound me . . .*
> *Of the Primal Spirit is my Substance, I am a wave*
> *In the river of Darkness and Light.*
> *The Maker of All Things is my Father and Mother,*
> *Heaven is my bed and Earth my cushion . . .*
> *With Nature my Substance is joined,*
> *I have no Passion, no Desire.*
> *Wash me and I shall be no whiter,*
> *Foul me and I shall yet be clean.*
> *I come not, yet am here;*
> *Hasten not, yet am swift.*

FRUIT NOT FLOWER

Higher Power
Is No-Power,
Is True Power.
Lesser Power
Does not Let Go,
Is not Power at all.
Higher Power
Does not Act,
And yet all is
Accomplished.
Lesser Power
Acts,
And fails to Accomplish.
Higher Benevolence
Acts with no purpose.
Righteousness
Acts with a purpose.
Ritual

Acts
And, when no one
Responds,
Rolls up its sleeves
To exert Force.
With loss of the Tao
Comes Power,
With loss of Power
Comes Benevolence,
With loss of Benevolence
Comes Righteousness.
With loss of Righteousness
Comes Ritual.
With Ritual
Trust is skin-deep,
The first step to Chaos.
Prophecy is a mere
Flower of the Tao,
The Beginning of Folly.
The Great Man
Dwells in Substance,
Not Surface,
Abides in Fruit,
Not Flower,
Eschews the latter,
Cleaves to the former.

THE RIVER MASTER

The Nameless Rulers of High Antiquity had Higher Power. And yet they can
be said to have had No-Power, since they never used their Power to instruct,
but instead followed Nature, the So-of-Itself, thereby Nourishing the True

Life-Destiny of the folk. Their Power was invisible. It was One with Heaven and Earth, it Harmonized with the Breath-Energy of All-under-Heaven, it helped the folk Attain Wholeness and Perfection Of-Themselves. Lesser Power is different: it never Lets Go.

> The Lesser Power
> Of Titles and Honors
> Is visible,
> It seeks Praise,
> Takes Credit.

Lesser Power is Action, gives Orders, Meddles, creates Name and Fame for itself. Prophecy is a mere Flower of the Tao. It has no Substance. It is the Beginning of Folly.

MAGISTER LIU

Higher Power and Higher Benevolence vary in degree, but they have this in common: they dwell in Substance, they abide in Fruit. Righteousness, Ritual, Clairvoyance, Prophecy, these vary in nature and quality, but they all have this in common: they dwell on the Surface, they abide in the Flower. Those who dwell in Substance and abide in Fruit are close to the Tao. Those who dwell on the Surface and abide in the Flower are estranged from the Tao. The Taoist dwells in the Wondrous Life of Nature, of the So-of-Itself, in which all Vain Thoughts are Transformed and become part of the Tao. This is the Art of the Tao. There is no Art other than this. As the Buddha said, this is the only Reality, all else is False and Unreal. All other ways of thinking are not the So-of-Itself. They do not have the Tao. When Self-Cultivation Attains Nature, the So-of-Itself, when the Taoist Lets Go, then all Returns Home to the One. This is the Higher Power.

Duyvendak: Higher Power that does not assert its Power is True Power. Lesser Power asserts itself and loses its True Character. Prophecy is the wish to know beforehand how the Tao is going to unfold. This Art of prognostication was much practiced in later, less pure forms of popular Taoism.

Chen: Lao-tzu regards the imposition of regulations and law, Ritual, as the first step toward Chaos.

Jia Yi (200–168 BC), "The Owl Rhapsody":

> *The Taoist*
> *Abandons things*
> *And cleaves to the Tao alone.*
> *The deluded Multitude*
> *Burden their Heart-and-Mind*
> *With Desire and Hate.*
> *The Taoist*
> *Is Clear and Still,*
> *Finds Peace in the Tao alone.*
> *The Taoist*
> *Is Vast and Empty,*
> *Swift and untrammeled,*
> *Transcends Self,*
> *Soaring on the wings of the Tao.*
> *The Taoist*
> *Discards Wisdom, forgets Form,*
> *Is borne on the Flood, sails forth,*
> *Resting on river islets.*
> *For the Taoist*
> *Life is a Floating,*
> *Death a Rest.*
> *The Taoist*
> *Is an unmoored boat,*
> *Drifting freely*
> *On deep still springs . . .*

THE ONE

Of those who Attained
The One
In Ancient Times:
Heaven Attained
The One through Clarity.
Earth Attained
The One through Calm.
Spirit Attained the One
And was Numinous.
The Valley Attained the One
And was Filled.
The Myriad Things
Attained the One
At Birth.
Nobles and Kings
Attained the One
And Set things Right
In All-under-Heaven.
It was through the One
That they were thus.
Heaven without Clarity
Would split asunder.
Earth without Calm

Would fall apart.
A Spirit not Numinous
Would fade.
A Valley not Filled
Would run dry.
The Myriad Things
Without Birth
Would be extinct.
Nobles and Kings
Without Esteem
Would tumble.
Esteem has its Root
In Humility,
In what is not Esteemed.
Height has its Foundation
In Depth.
Nobles and Kings
Call themselves
Orphaned and Destitute.
Humility is their Root.
The greatest number of Carriages
Is No-Carriage.
Do not tinkle like Jade:
Rumble like Rock,
Attain the One.

THE RIVER MASTER

To Attain the One is Non-Action, it is to be a Child of the Tao.

Heaven Attained
The One,

Suspending
Clarity and Pure Light
In the Firmament.
Earth Attained
The One,
Achieving
Unshaken Calm.
Spirit Attained
The One
And had Numinous Power.

The Valley Attained the One and had Infinite Capacity to be Filled. The Myriad Things Attained the One, the Tao, and were Born. Kings Attained the One and Ruled All-under-Heaven in Peace.

MAGISTER LIU

Wholeness is Achieved
By Attaining
The One.
Without the One,
Things Fail.

The One is the True Breath-Energy contained within the Supreme Ultimate, it is the Mother of the Myriad Things, it is itself without Form but sets Form in Motion. The One enables everything to be what it is—Heaven, Earth, Spirit, the Valley. Without the One, Kings lose Authority, they Tumble, however high their Rank. The One is Root and Foundation of all. Kings call themselves Orphans and Waifs, out of Humility. The Tao, the Root of all, is enjoyed by every one of the Myriad Things through Attainment of the One, just as many Carriages have as their Root No-Carriage at all. Their Usefulness lies in the Empty Space, in Non-Being.

Put Jade
Out of mind,
Return to Rock,

To the One,
Most precious thing of all,
Mystery of Mysteries,
Gateway to All Marvels,
Ancestor of the Myriad Things.

Chen: The One, the Absoluteness and Universality of the Tao, is a necessary condition for the Existence of all things, beyond numbers or enumeration; it is the sustaining factor of the Essence of each thing. The Valley being Filled is perhaps an allusion to the womb, and its procreative function.

Duyvendak: The One which is the theme of this Chapter is the Tao, by which everything is supported. Man and World form a fundamental Unity. All things are indissolubly interrelated and naturally influence each other.

Chan: The One is Unity and Simplicity, the Uncarved Block before it split up into individual things. It is things "merged into One," the Beginning and Origin of things, the synthesis of all contraries, opposites, and distinctions.

Waley: Their [Numinous] Holiness—their *ling*—is to Spirit and to spirits (or objects and animals "possessed" by Spirit or spirits) what Power is to man. It is cognate to words meaning life, name, command, etc.

The Book of Taoist Master Zhuang:
Chapter 5:

> If we look at things in terms of their Difference, then we have the body's liver and gall, we have the two southern states of Chu and Yue. But if we look at things in terms of their Sameness, then the Myriad Things are all One. Whosoever sees things in this light can set Heart-and-Mind free to roam in the Harmony of Inner Power.

Chapter 11:

> I hold on to the One, I abide in its Harmony, and therefore have kept myself alive for twelve thousand years. And never has my body suffered Decay.

Chapter 22:

> The Myriad Things are the One . . . The Breath-Energy of the One
> Connects All-under-Heaven. The Taoist prizes the One.

Su Dongpo dedicated a poem to an Abbot, imbuing it with Taoist Intimations
of the One—One Moon reflected many times in the river.

I leave behind the River Huai,
I enter the River Luo,
The land grows dusty.
I raise my fan
Against the west wind,
Which seeks to coat me with dirt,
And marvel
At the cloudy mountains
Never changing color,
At the one moon
Reflected a thousand times.
For one who has a peaceful
Heart-and-Mind,
Who enjoys Harmony
With the Tao,
Old age is a fine thing.
Objects encountered
Without Emotion
Engender
Fresh lines of verse . . .

TURNING

Turning is the Motion
Of the Tao,
Its Practice
Is Soft.
In All-under-Heaven
The Myriad Things are Born
From Being.
Being is Born
From Non-Being.

THE RIVER MASTER

The Turning of the Tao gives Birth to the Myriad Things. To ignore this Root is to Perish. The Practice of the Tao is Soft and Gentle, it leads to Endurance and Long Life.

From Heaven and Earth
To Spirit Light,
Every flying and creeping thing
Is Born
From the Tao,
Which is itself
Without Form.
They are Born
From Non-Being.

MAGISTER LIU

To Know the One
Is to be One
With the Primal Mother
Of Life-Destiny,
To witness
The Radiance and Marvel
Of Breath-Energy.
To Turn,
To be Soft,
It is to Return
From Being
To Non-Being.

Non-Being is the Tao. When the Uncarved Block Before-Heaven split apart, the Falsity of Latter-Heaven emerged, the Cycle of Yin and Yang began. The Hard and the Strong are prized by the Multitude, their Heart-and-Mind filled with Thoughts and Cares. When the Heart-and-Mind is entangled with Love and encumbered with Emotion, when it seems impossible to Turn, to Attain the One, then one must nevertheless Turn to the furthest limit of Turning, to where no further Turning is possible, one must be Soft to the ultimate degree of Softness. This is to Attain the One, to attain Purity, to enter the Realm where there is no Two, where Truth is One with the Tao, where Outer Radiance and Inner Marvel merge.

> The Seeker of the Tao
> Turns through Softness
> To the One,
> Returns Home
> To Non-Being,
> To the Formless,
> To Long Life.

Duyvendak: Turning is the constant alternation of Being and Non-Being, Flourishing and Decay. Things always Turn in this direction, in reverse.

Chen: Lao-tzu emphasizes the eventual Return of things to their point of departure, which is the Tao. This is a Return to the original state of Calm and Emptiness.

The Buddhist monk Sun Chuo (314–371), in his Rhapsody "Wandering on Mount Tiantai," traces the Turnings, the Inner Pilgrimage of the spiritual aspirant, in an allegorical "ascent" of the crags of the Tiantai mountains up into a Realm beyond Being and Non-Being. Sun Chuo blends Buddhist and Taoist notions of transcendence in rhapsodic lines that foreshadow the lengthy improvisations of our eighteenth-century Commentator Magister Liu.

> *Cleaving to*
> *The Dark and Hidden Tao,*
> *I trudge the steepest slopes*
> *Which are level plains to me.*
> *And when I have traversed*

Their Nine Turns,
The road stretches on
Before me
Unending and Clear,
And my Heart-and-Mind
Wanders,
Unconcerned.
My eyes roam free,
My slow steps take me
Where they will.
And then when I have Turned,
When I have come full circle
In my wanderings,
When Body is Stilled,
And Heart-and-Mind at Rest . . .
Then I chant
In a clear voice
By the endless river . . .
Abandoning both Being
And Non-Being,
That spring from a single Source.
I chatter merrily
All day long,
As if in Utter Silence,
As if I'd never spoken.
In deepest Contemplation,
I merge
With the Myriad Images,
Merging Self
With the So-of-Itself.

THE DARK LIGHT

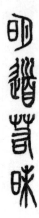

The Highest
Hear the Tao,
And live it
To the full.
The Middling
Hear the Tao,
And it seems
Now here, now gone.
The Lowest
Hear the Tao,
And laugh
Outright;
Their laughter testifies
To the Tao.
An old saying goes:
"The Light of the Tao
Seems Dark.

To Advance in the Tao
Seems like a Retreat.
The Smooth Path
Of the Tao
Seems Pitted."
The Highest Power
Is like a Valley.
The Purest White
Seems Sullied.
Ample Power
Seems Flimsy.
Established Power
Seems Thin,
Truest Power
Seems Empty.
The Great Square
Has no Corners.
The Great Vessel
Is Completed
Slowly.
Great Music
Is Faint.
The Great Image
Has no Form.
The Tao is Hidden,
Incognito,
It has no Name.
It Gives,
It Completes.

THE RIVER MASTER

The Highest simply
Live the Tao.
The Middling strive to
Practice Self-Cultivation,
But are from time to time
Distracted by Wealth,
By Beauty, Splendor, and Honors,
They are assailed by Doubt,
Deluded by Desire.
The Lowest
Laugh out loud,
Despising the Tao
As Soft,
Mocking its Simplicity
As Vulgar.

There is a saying:

To seek the True Light
Of the Tao
Is to search in the Dark.
To Reach the Tao
Is to Retreat.

The Taoist of Highest Power is like a Deep Valley, unashamed of the Silt in the Riverbed. The Taoist of Great Inner Purity may appear sullied by dirt, is not resplendent. The Taoist of Ample Power may seem foolish and inadequate. Established Power and Truest Substance are like a Color that has faded and lost its Brilliance, like a Square with No Corners. They may be stolen away at any moment, leaving nothing but a Void. The Great Vessel of the Tao, like one of the Nine Great Tripods or like a fine bowl fashioned out of coral, cannot be quickly Completed.

Great Music,
Like rumbling thunder,
Bides its time,

Saves its breath,
Says little.

MAGISTER LIU

This Giving, this Completion, this Vessel of the Tao, are the result of gradual Self-Cultivation, of sustained Generosity of Spirit, they are not something Achieved through Impulse or Desire. The Twelve Hidden Qualities (the Dark Light, the Retreat, the Pitted Path, and so on) are discovered in the course of diligent Seeking. They are parts of its Mystery. The Tao's Motion is a Turning, it is Soft. But for Seekers of the Tao to Turn, to be Truly Soft, first they must be Illumined by the Dark Light of the Tao. The Highest receive the Tao at once into their Innermost Heart-and-Mind. They can Advance steadily in Self-Cultivation even though it may feel like a Slow Retreat. As for the Middling, they may grasp the Words of the Tao but not their meaning, they may sense a Savor within the Blandness of the Tao, but be unable to Understand why it is so. They vacillate between Trust and Disbelief, between Diligence and Indolence, and sometimes lose their way. The Lowest burst out laughing at the Tao's Blandness and lack of Savor, which they find Vulgar. They prize that which is Strange and Difficult, whereas the Tao is Simple and Easy.

The Taoists
Never speak glibly
Of the Tao.
Its Light
Glows Darkly
Through their Words.
The Tao is a Great Square
Without Corners,
Unconstrained,
Radiant and Pure,
Naked and Free as an Infant.

The Great Vessel of Self-Cultivation cannot be Attained in the work of a morning or an evening. It is the result of Courage and Perseverance over days and years.

Its Completion is slow.
This is the Great Music
Of the Tao,
Too Faint to be heard.
The Tao itself is
Silence.

Wilhelm: Virtues in their highest form do nothing to put themselves in the limelight. The Great Quadrant [Square] has no corners because it is of Infinite Size and therefore eludes perception, just as the Silence of Great Music exceeds the range of what is audible.

Xi Kang, in a letter to his friend Shan Tao, another of the Seven Sages of the Bamboo Grove, explains his refusal to take office, his firm resolve to keep his Light Dark, to Retreat into a life of Retirement.

My taste for independence has intensified of late from my reading of two books, *The Book of Taoist Master Zhuang* and *The Tao and the Power*. As a result, any Desire for Fame I may have had has grown daily weaker, and my commitment to freedom increasingly stronger. The wild deer, if captured young and reared in captivity, may become docile and obedient, but if caught full-grown, it will stare wildly and butt against its bonds, it will dash into boiling water or fire in order to escape. Such is the case with me. You may dress the deer up with a golden bridle, you may feed it delicacies, but it will only long the more for its native woods and yearn for rich pasture . . . If I were now to enter official life, how could I avoid getting into trouble with the authorities? Besides, I have studied the esoteric lore of the Taoist Masters, whereby a man's life can be indefinitely prolonged through eating certain herbs, and I firmly believe this to be true. To wander among hills and streams, observing fish and birds, this is something I would have to give up forthwith. Why should I relinquish what gives me pleasure for something that fills me with dread? Of late I have been studying the techniques of Longevity, I have cast out all ideas of Fame and Glory, I have let my Heart-and-Mind wander in

Calm. What I value most of all is Non-Action . . . Today I only wish to stay on in this out-of-the-way lane and bring up my children and grandchildren, on occasion relaxing and reminiscing with old friends—a cup of unstrained wine, a song to the accompaniment of my Lute—this is the sum of my ambitions.

ONE, TWO, THREE

The Tao gave Birth
To the One.
The One gave Birth
To the Two.
The Two gave Birth
To the Three.
The Three gave Birth
To the Myriad Things,
Which carry Yin
On their backs
And Embrace Yang,
Harmonized
By the Breath-Energy
Of Emptiness.
The Multitude
Hate to be Orphans,
To be Solitary and Destitute;
But Kings and Princes
Call themselves
By these very Names.
Things Diminish

And Increase,
They Increase
And Diminish.
Others Teach this,
I also Teach it.
"The Violent do not die
A natural death."
This is the Father
Of my Teaching.

THE RIVER MASTER

Some Teach Others to abandon the Soft for the Hard. I Teach them to abandon Violence, to abandon the Hard and Cleave to the Soft. The Violent do not Trust in Deep Mysteries, they rebel against the Tao and the Power, they do not follow the True Teaching.

MAGISTER LIU

The Tao gave Birth
To the One,
Mother
Of the Myriad Things,
Which Diminish and Increase,
But which never stray
From the One,
From the Emptiness
Of Non-Being.
The Tao gave Birth
To the Breath-Energy
Of the One,

The Beginning,
The First Spring of Life.
The Cycle of the Tao
Never ends,
It never strays
From the One.

Duyvendak: The One, the Unity, of the Tao operates through the duality of Yin and Yang. Yin is the dark, cold, feminine, passive category. Yang is the light, warm, masculine, active category. The Three probably refers to Heaven, Earth, and Man. From these Three, all things, the Myriad Things, proceed.

The *Classic of the Plain Girl*: Between Heaven and Earth, all Movement follows the interaction of Yin and Yang. Yang attains Yin and is thereby Transformed, Yin Attains Yang and is thereby Connected.

The *I Ching*, the Great Treatise: When Yin and Yang Energies join, when Hard and Soft unite, then is Substance Attained. One Yin, One Yang! They need each other, they work together. Know this Tao, and you will be happy and strong! You will Live Long, and be Beautiful!

Waley: The Myriad Things are a mixture of Hard and Soft, Light and Dark, etc. To be a Prince is a "sunny," Yang, thing as opposed to a "shady," Yin, thing. But a Prince does not feel properly Harmonized unless he also carries "the shade of Yin at his back," which he obtains by humbling himself, giving himself humble titles such as Orphan and Destitute.

Su Dongpo, in his poem "Studio Inscription," writes of the Calm to be found in the Mirror of No-Self.

Great Calamity
Stems from
Possession of a Body.
With no Body,
There is no illness.

With Calm,
Complete Illumination
Dawns
Of-Itself,
Mirror upon Mirror—
The Mirror of No-Self;
Water cleansed with Water,
Two Waters,
One Purity.
One Vast Heart
Between Heaven and Earth,
Alone,
Upright.

THE SOFTEST THING

The Softest Thing
In All-under-Heaven
Outstrips
The Hardest.
Non-Being
Enters No-Space.
I Know the Benefit
Of Non-Action,
The Wordless Teaching.
Few in All-under-Heaven
Attain it.

THE RIVER MASTER

The Softest is Water, the Hardest is Metal and Stone. Water bores its way through the Strong and the Hard, it penetrates all.

> The Tao
> Is Non-Being,
> It has neither Form
> Nor Substance.
> It comes and goes,
> It departs from and enters into
> No-Space.
> It Connects
> With the Light of Spirit,
> It Nourishes
> Every living creature.

The Tao is Non-Action. With it the Myriad Things are Transformed, they become effortlessly Whole, in accord with the So-of-Itself. This is the True Benefit of Non-Action, this is the Soft and Gentle Tao, a Wordless Teaching learned from Self-Cultivation. When the Nation is Ruled through Non-Action, the Myriad Folk will Benefit, they will no longer suffer and toil. But few Rulers in All-under-Heaven Attain this, few Rule Self or Nation through Non-Action.

MAGISTER LIU

> In the Non-Action
> Of the Tao,
> The Soft
> Outstrips the Hard,
> The Clumsy
> Are Masters
> Of the Cunning,
> Fools are Masters

Of the "wise."

Waley: To yield is to conquer, to grasp is to lose. The soft, the unassertive, the inconspicuous, the lowly, the imperfect, the incomplete are symbols of the Primal Stuff that underlies the kaleidoscope of the apparent Universe.

The poet Tao Yuanming was aware of the Wordless Teaching, he knew how hard it is to find Words for the "Tao that cannot be told," that can only be experienced.

> *The mountain is fine*
> *At evening of the day,*
> *Birds fly Home together.*
> *Within these things*
> *There is a hint of Truth,*
> *But if I try to tell it,*
> *I cannot find the Words.*

SUFFICIENCY

Which is Dearer:
Name
Or True Person?
Which means more:
Person or Property?
Which causes greater Harm:
Gain or Loss?
Undue Love
Comes at Great Cost.
Hoarding entails
Heavy Loss.
To Know Sufficiency
Averts Disgrace;
Whosoever Knows
When to Halt
Averts Misfortune,
Endures.

THE RIVER MASTER

Pursuit of Name and Fame relegates True Person to second place. To Crave Property Harms the Person. Pursuit of Gain injures Life. Undue Love of Sensual Beauty and Pleasure wastes the Spirit. Wealth invites Misfortune, inciting Robbers to ransack the Warehouse, to rifle the Grave.

> Whosoever does not
> Pursue Gain,
> And knows Content,
> Is free of Desire,
> Incurs
> Neither Harm
> Nor Disgrace.

To Know when to Halt, to be disentangled from Gain, to be unperturbed by the Senses, is to avoid Peril, is to befriend Fortune. Self-Cultivation keeps the Spirit Safe from Harm.

MAGISTER LIU

Those who Know Sufficiency, who Know when to Halt and not to Waver, will experience neither Disgrace nor Misfortune. Their Person and their Heart-and-Mind will be at Peace, they will Thrive and Endure. Theirs is the Tao and the Power, they will accrue Inner Wealth.

> The Desire
> To Accumulate,
> To Hoard Property,
> The Desire for Glory,
> These are
> False Wealth,
> Counterfeit Coin.

This is to relegate Life-Destiny to second place. It is to Crave a Small Gain at Great Cost. The Seeker of the Tao Cherishes Inner Sufficiency and

Contentment, and Knows when to call a Halt. This is an Honest Economy of Spirit, a Heart-and-Mind of Integrity and Calm. It Nurtures Breath-Energy, it Endures in All-under-Heaven.

Duyvendak: If one does not attempt to thwart the natural development of things [if one Knows when to Halt], it is possible to complete one's own natural course of life [one Endures].

Tao Yuanming, reluctantly on his way back to an official post, meditates in plain language on the perpetual dilemma of the would-be Recluse, who seeks to Know when to Halt.

> *Preoccupied with my mission,*
> *I cannot sleep.*
> *At midnight*
> *The lone boat*
> *Wends its way.*
> *I care not for Preferment,*
> *But yearn to plow my fields,*
> *To quit my job and go Home—*
> *I have no love of Rank.*
> *To Cultivate the True Tao*
> *In my humble cottage*
> *Is my highest Aspiration.*

FLAWED PERFECTION

Great Perfection
Seems Flawed,
But its Practice
Never Fades.
Great Plenitude
Seems Empty,
But its Practice is
Never Exhausted.
Great Straightness
Seems Curved,
Great Cleverness
Seems Clumsy,
Great Eloquence
Seems to Stammer.
Movement Prevails
Over Cold,
Calm Prevails

Over Heat.
Clarity and Calm
Set All-under-Heaven
To Rights.

THE RIVER MASTER

A Ruler Perfect
In the Tao and the Power
Seems Flawed,
Puts aside
Name and Fame,
Buries Praise.
The Taoist seems Flawed
But Attains the Perfection
Of the Moment,
And is never exhausted.

MAGISTER LIU

With Calm and Clarity, Selfish Thoughts and Desires diminish.

This is to Practice
Non-Action,
To be Busy
About No-Business,
The So-of-Itself.
This is Natural Imperfection,
Natural Emptiness,
It is to be
Naturally Curved,
Naturally Clumsy,

> To Stammer,
> But never to Fade.

The Taoist, however Clear and Calm he may be, Knows his own Insufficiency, his own Imperfection. The Taoist seems Imperfect, but contains a Deeper Perfection. The Taoist Returns Home to Non-Action, to the Inexhaustible. This is the Great Perfection, which sets All-under-Heaven to Rights, which sets the Person to Rights. The Taoist Cleaves to the True Breath-Energy of the Tao, which fills the Universe.

> I am the Tao,
> The Tao is Me.

Waley (quoting *The Book of Taoist Master Zhuang*): To a mind that is still, the whole Universe surrenders.

In the closing pages of the great eighteenth-century masterpiece of fiction *The Story of the Stone*, the reader is reminded that one of the main functions of the novel is to transmit the Taoist message, that things are not as they seem, that the Eloquent may Stammer, that Perfection may seem Flawed, that Truth is Fiction, Fiction Truth. In this lies the One, the Reconciliation and Harmony of so-called Opposites.

> The Extraordinary and the Ordinary, Truth and Fiction, are all relative to each other. Perhaps fellow humans whom the dream of life has ensnared may find in this tale an echo, may be summoned back by it to their True Home; while free spirits of the high hills may find in the record of Brother Stone's Transformations a reflected light to quicken their own aspirations.

ENDURING CONTENTMENT

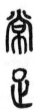

When the Tao
Rules
All-under-Heaven,
Swift Horses
Fertilize the fields.
When the Tao is absent
From All-under-Heaven,
War Horses
Are bred on the Altar-Meads.
The Greatest Calamity
Is Discontent,
The Greatest Harm
Is the Desire
To Acquire and Achieve.
True Contentment,
Sure Knowledge
Of Sufficiency,
These Endure.

THE RIVER MASTER

In times of Peace and the Tao, swift War Horses are put out to pasture, they fertilize the fields. Likewise, by quietly Practicing Self-Cultivation in Clarity and Calm, the individual preserves Yang Essence and enriches the Person. But when a Ruler lacks the Tao, and War knows no restraint, then War Horses are reared in the Altar-Meads reserved for Ritual Ceremonies and are then dispatched to the field of battle. The Greatest Ill is Desire, the Craving of the Senses. The Greatest Calamity is Discontent, the relentless Pursuit of Wealth and Rank. The Greatest Harm stems from Greed and Ambition.

> To know
> Contentment,
> To maintain a Heart-and-Mind
> Free of Desire,
> Is to preserve
> The True Root.

MAGISTER LIU

Attainment of the Tao depends on Knowing Sufficiency, on being Content with one's Lot. Whosoever is Content is safe from Calamity and Harm.

> When All-under-Heaven
> Is Ruled by the Tao,
> Swift and gorgeously caparisoned
> War Horses
> Are simple beasts
> To fertilize the soil,
> Not creatures to be sent into battle.
> But when there is
> No Trust,
> No Tao
> In All-under-Heaven,
> When the True is forsaken
> For the False,

When Victory, Force, and Contending
Are given preference,
Then War Horses
Are bred on the Altar-Meads,
Troops are marshaled,
Weapons of war deployed.
Then Calm and Clarity
Quit the Heart-and-Mind,
And Thoughts of Desire arise,
With Delusions
Of Ambition and Greed.
Passion runs riot,
And all manner of
Cunning schemes
Are Born
Within the Heart-and-Mind,
Turning Life
Topsy-turvy.
Every Ill, Calamity, and Harm
Has its origin in this.

Duyvendak: Fleet horses used for war-chariots are unharnessed because there is no more War, and the only remaining interest in these beautiful animals is for the sake of their dung, which may be used as manure on the land. On the contrary, if the Tao is not followed, one thinks of nothing but War, and War Horses are even raised on the sacred ground where stood the altars for the sacrifices to Heaven and Earth.

Of all China's poets, the one who exhibits Enduring Contentment most memorably is surely Tao Yuanming, the Gentleman of the Five Willow Trees, as he calls himself in this brief autobiographical sketch, written when he was still a young man.

I don't know where this gentleman was born and I am not sure of his name, but beside his house were five willow trees, from which he took his nickname. He was of a placid and calm disposition and rarely spoke. He had no envy of Fame or Fortune. He was fond of reading, without puzzling greatly over difficult passages. When he came across something to his liking he would be so delighted he would forget his meals. By nature he liked wine, but being poor he could not always afford it. Knowing his circumstances, his friends and relatives would invite him over when they had a bottle. He never drank without emptying his cup, and always ended up tipsy, after which he would retire, unconcerned about the future. He lived alone in a bare hut, which gave no adequate shelter against rain and sun. His short coat was torn and patched, his cooking pots were frequently empty, but he was unperturbed. He wrote poems for his own amusement, and in them can be seen something of his innermost thoughts. He had no concern for worldly success, and so he ended his days.

TO KNOW WITHOUT GOING

Without setting foot
Outside the door,
The Taoist Knows
All-under-Heaven;
Without looking
Through the window,
The Taoist sees
The Tao of Heaven-and-Nature.
The further one goes,
The less one Knows.
The Taoist Knows
Without going,
Understands
Without seeing,
Accomplishes
Without Action.

THE RIVER MASTER

The Tao
Of Heaven-and-Nature
And the Tao
Of the Person
Are One.
Heaven and Man
Are Connected,
Their Breath-Energy
Is Linked.

The Taoist, without rising to the Heights of Heaven, without sinking into the Abyss, without going anywhere, Knows All-under-Heaven, Understands it in the Heart-and-Mind. If the Ruler loves the Tao, his subjects will love the Inner Power. If the Ruler loves War, his subjects will love Force. The True Taoist examines that which is within in order to Understand that which is without.

MAGISTER LIU

The Heart-and-Mind contains All-under-Heaven, the Person contains the Myriad Things. The True Breath-Energy of the Person is the True Breath-Energy of All-under-Heaven. They are One and the Same. What need is there to step outside the door, what need is there to look through the window, in order to Understand the Tao of Heaven-and-Nature?

That would be
To abandon
What is close at hand
For something
That is distant.

The Taoist Vision comes from Observation of the Outer Radiance, and from Contemplation of the Inner Marvel, from Non-Action. There is no need of Action, no need to go anywhere. A Knowledge of Sufficiency is Acquired without setting foot outside the door, the Tao of Heaven-and-Nature can be seen without looking through the window. Even if one sets foot outside, one can Know only that which one has already experienced. Looking through the window, one can see only that which has Form, not that which is without Form. The further into the distance one travels, the more one leaves behind that which is close at hand, the more one is removed from the Inner Vision, from the Tao, the more one loses sight of that which is Truly Great. One ends up Knowing and Understanding less.

> The Taoist sees
> With the Vision of Spirit,
> Darkly One
> With the Tao
> Of Heaven-and-Nature.
> The Taoist Understands everything
> With the Inner Eye,
> Sees the Tao everywhere,
> In everything.
> To see this
> Requires no Effort,
> No Action.
> It is perfected
> In Silence,
> In True Union
> With the Tao.

Waley: The further one travels "away from the Tao," the further one moves away from Unity into Multiplicity.

The Complete Reality Taoist Qiu Chuji (1148–1227) describes an Astral Being whose Inner Vision transcends the bounds of normal perception.

> *The Sylph of the Grotto*
> *Cries out*
> *The name of Lao-tzu,*

Essence
Of Luminous Energy
Floating
In Splendor and Solitude.
From its exalted Height
The Sylph gazes down
On an Azure Sea,
Guarding an unruffled Silence
In the white clouds.

DECREASE

Studying
Requires Daily Increase.
The Tao
Requires Daily Decrease,
Decrease upon Decrease,
Until Non-Action is Attained.
With Non-Action
Everything is Accomplished,
Everything Happens.
All-under-Heaven is won
Through No-Business.
Meddling never wins
All-under-Heaven.

THE RIVER MASTER

Studying means applying oneself to such subjects as the Rites and Music. This requires Daily Increase, Daily Effort. By contrast, the natural Tao of the So-of-Itself calls for Daily Decrease in Passion and Desire, their gradual extinction, until:

> Non-Action is Attained,
> One is quiet
> As a Child,
> Undertaking nothing,
> And Inner Power
> Is One with the Tao.

When Busy-Bodies Rule, they indoctrinate and harass the folk, who enjoy no Peace. They never succeed in winning their allegiance.

MAGISTER LIU

This Decrease is Daily Decrease in Action, until Non-Action is Attained and the True Principle of Heaven-and-Nature Flows in an effortless and inscrutable stream. The Illumined Taoist Knows without needing to travel, Understands without needing to see, Accomplishes all through Non-Action. At a lesser level, ordinary study is still needed. This is followed by a progression from Action to Non-Action, from Observation of Outer Radiance to Contemplation of Inner Marvel. This initial studying does require Daily Increase, a gradual development. True Self-Cultivation in the Tao itself, by contrast, is a matter of Daily Decrease.

> A reduction,
> A shrinking,
> A gradual diminution
> In the Heart-and-Mind.

At Birth humans are all endowed with the Primal Before-Heaven Breath of Yang Energy, with Inner Power, their portion from the Inchoate Primordial

Chaos. Then the Breath-Energy of After-Heaven gradually encroaches upon them, and the Original True Energy slowly fades.

Bit by bit
The Human Heart-and-Mind
Waxes,
While the True Heart-and-Mind of the Tao
Wanes,
Day after day,
Year after year,
And distance from the Tao
Grows ever greater.

But with Self-Cultivation, the Desire of the Human Heart-and-Mind Decreases, and the Heart-and-Mind of the Tao Increases. This is a Return to the Root, to the Non-Action of the So-of-Itself, purified of all dregs. This is the Inner Transformation of Self-Cultivation.

Chen: Studying means the Pursuit of the differentiated Knowledge of external phenomena. This becomes increasingly complex and confusing. The Self-Cultivation of the Tao is an experience of Intuitive Understanding through which an undifferentiated wholeness is Attained.

Duyvendak: This Chapter is a very clear statement of Non-Action.

Meng Jiao (751–814) reflects from his mountaintop on the futility of studying Books and the vanity of pursuing Fame.

South Mountain
Fills Heaven and Earth,
Sun and Moon
Are Born from the rocks.
There is majesty in the tall peaks
As night falls,
And at dawn

A soft light in the deep valleys.
Here in the mountains
Men find Truth.
The trail is steep,
But the Heart-and-Mind
Grows Calm.
Strong winds
Buffet the pines and cypresses,
Their sound sweeps the gullies clean.
Here I have come to regret
Having studied Books,
Day after day,
In search of Empty Fame.

QUIET AND SELF-EFFACING

The Taoist has
No Heart-and-Mind,
But regards the Heart-and-Mind
Of the common folk
As his own, saying:
"I consider the Good
To be Good,
The Not-Good
I also consider Good."
This is the True Goodness
Of Inner Power.
"Those of Good Faith
I have Faith in,
I also have Faith
In the Faithless."
This is the True Good Faith
Of Inner Power.
In All-under-Heaven
The True Taoist
Is Quiet and Self-Effacing,
Keeps Heart-and-Mind
Inchoate

For the sake of
All-under-Heaven.
The Hundred Families
Strain their eyes and ears,
The Taoist
Regards them all
As Children.

THE RIVER MASTER

When the folk lack Good Faith, the Inner Power of the Taoist can Transform them and cause them to have Good Faith.

The Taoist Rules
All-under-Heaven,
Quietly,
With the Heart-and-Mind
Of a Fool.

The common folk strain their ears and eyes to see and hear the Taoist, who loves them as Children, Nurturing them and expecting no reward.

MAGISTER LIU

Forgetting the Heart-and-Mind of Me, keeping the Heart-and-Mind Inchoate in the Tao, the Taoist sees all generously through the eyes of Goodness and Good Faith, through the Inner Power of the Tao.

Each individual is
A Child to be Nurtured,
An Infant to be Cherished.
Absence of
Human Heart-and-Mind
Brings a Great Communality,
A Generosity of Spirit,
Vast as Heaven and Earth.

> There is no Me,
> All is shared among all.
> The Taoist
> Nurtures this shared Root.
> All is seen as Good,
> In the Light
> Of Inner Power.

All incline their eyes and ears, they listen with respect and reverence, they Resonate, and in Resonating are Transformed. They emulate the Inchoate Heart-and-Mind of the Taoist, they are spiritually Connected. It is a Spiritual Communion, from the So-of-Itself, without Force or Effort.

Duyvendak: The Taoist has no fixed views [no Heart-and-Mind]. He is morally indifferent. He admits both Good and Evil equally, and maintains the same conduct towards all men. His Heart-and-Mind is completely free from prejudice [it is Inchoate].

Meng Haoran (ca. 689–740) finds Calm (and a touch of Taoist Melancholy) when waiting for his friend at sunset.

> *The sun sets*
> *On the western hills,*
> *Quickly the valleys*
> *Darken.*
> *The moon rises through the pines,*
> *In the chill of night,*
> *Amid the crystal sounds*
> *Of wind and stream.*
> *The woodcutters*
> *Have all gone Home,*
> *In the mist the birds*
> *Are settling in their nests.*
> *My friend promised to join me tonight.*
> *Alone with my Lute*
> *I wait on the vine-strewn path.*

NO TERRAIN OF DEATH

There is a Coming
Into Life,
An Entering
Into Death.
The Companions of Life
Make up one third.
The Companions of Death
Another third.
The final third
Have their Heart-and-Mind
Too set on Living,
They slide from Life
To the Terrain of Death.
I have heard that
Those who Truly Nurture Life
Travel on Land
Without encountering
Rhinoceros or Tiger,

They join the Fray of War
Without wearing Armor
Or bearing Arms.
The Rhinoceros finds
Nowhere to butt,
The Tiger
Nowhere to dig its claws,
The Enemy
Nowhere to drive the points
Of its Weapons.
For those
Who Truly Nurture Life
There is
No Terrain of Death.

THE RIVER MASTER

Whosoever clings to Life and sets too much store by living loses the Thread of the Tao, wantonly defies Heaven-and-Nature. Whosoever Nurtures Life through Self-Cultivation, such a one follows Heaven-and-Nature, the So-of-Itself, and is safe from Harm. Wild beasts have no cause to do Harm, the Enemy has no reason to attack. For these there is no Terrain of Death.

MAGISTER LIU

Death and No-Death exist within the Heart-and-Mind. That is their Terrain. A Heart-and-Mind that clings to Life at all costs is Filled with Fear of Death, and so enters the Terrain of Death. But those who Nurture True Life, who practice Self-Cultivation in the True Tao, have no Fear of Death.

Neither wild beast
Nor armed Enemy

Can Harm
Inviolable Inner Natures
Such as these.
And so
In Death
They do not Die,
For them
There is
No Terrain of Death.

In Life, plants and insects Flow with the unfolding of Life. In Death, they
Flow with the unfolding of Death. Some humans deny the Flow of Life and
Death. In living they cling to Life, to Fame and Wealth.

They crave Life
And speed
Toward Death.

For those who Nurture True Life, who practice Self-Cultivation in the Tao,
there is no Me, and therefore no Other. They walk the Earth Safe from Harm,
they do not step onto the Terrain of Death. The secret of No-Mind is the
Nourishment of Non-Being, seeing Life as No-Life. The Terrain of Death is
within. Life and Death proceed from the Heart-and-Mind. Within the Human Heart-and-Mind, the Terrain of Life becomes the Terrain of Death.
Where there is No Human Heart-and-Mind:

The Terrain of Death
Is the Terrain of Life.
There is a never-ending
Flow of Life.
This is Long Life.

JM: Here the River Master and Magister Liu interpret the text quite differ-
ently. I have omitted a large part of the River Master's Commentary, not
wishing to cause confusion. As I see it, this Chapter (which has given rise to
widely varying interpretations) is saying that we can divide humans into

three categories: (1) the young (the recently Born) and energetic (Duyvendak: those on the ascent); (2) the old and declining (those past their zenith); and (3) those between Youth and Old Age, who cling to Life (they think too much of unnatural devices to protect Life and arrive at the opposite result).

Wilhelm: In their striving and yearning for Life, these [the third category] make themselves vulnerable to Death.

Chan: Ignorant followers of the Taoist religion thought themselves protected from Death. The most notorious example of this was that of the Boxers (*Yihetuan*), who actually believed that through magic and superstitious practices they could make their bodies immune to the bullets of the European soldiers.

Lu You (1125–1210), himself a Taoist alchemist, writes of joining an old Taoist Hermit, to Nurture Life in his retreat.

> *The Green Goat Taoist*
> *Dwells among bamboos,*
> *Plants flowers*
> *From his old Temple in the capital.*
> *As the light rain clears,*
> *He watches the cranes dance.*
> *In the quiet outside his window,*
> *He hears the bees drone.*
> *In his alchemical furnace*
> *The coals glow warmly,*
> *His tipsy sleeves*
> *Flutter in the breeze.*
> *I have come here,*
> *Dismissed from office,*
> *Free of care,*
> *To share your simple life.*

MYSTIC POWER

The Tao
Gives Birth,
The Power
Nurtures.
Matter
Creates Form,
Potential Energy
Completes.
Each one
Of the Myriad Things
Reveres the Tao,
Prizes the Inner Power.
There is no Decree
For the Tao to Give Birth,
For the Power to Nurture,
These things happen Of-Themselves.
The Tao gives Birth,
The Power Nurtures,
Rears,
Fulfills,
Feeds,

Shelters.
The Tao gives Birth
But never Possesses.
The Taoist Acts
Without Attachment,
Leads
But never takes charge.
This is Mystic Power.

THE RIVER MASTER

Inner Power spreads Breath-Energy, it Nourishes things, and gives them
Form and Image. Its Potential Energy Completes them. The Tao issues no
Edicts, the Myriad Things Resonate Of-Themselves, like shadow or echo. The
Tao brings their Life-Destiny to Completion.

The Tao
Makes things grow,
But does not control.
This is its Mystic Power—
Compassionate,
Dark,
Invisible.

MAGISTER LIU

Mystic Power is the
Inner Power
Of Primal Radiance,
Gateway to All Marvels.

It cannot be seen, it cannot be Known, it cannot be Named. If we have to give it a Name, we call it the So-of-Itself, we call it Nature. For Seekers of the Tao, who Nurture Life, there is no Terrain of Death.

> Inner Power,
> Mystic Power
> In its Non-Being,
> In its Non-Action,
> Is invisible,
> Is unknowable,

It Nourishes, it brings to Fulfillment, to Completion.

> The Seekers
> Return to Nature,
> To the So-of-Itself.

The Myriad Things are Nurtured, Reared, brought to Completion, Sheltered by the Inner Power, the Mother, the Outer Radiance. The Power itself has no Form, it is only to be seen in the Growth and Fulfillment of the Myriad Things.

Chen: The Tao and the Power are revered by the Myriad Things because they do not interfere with the individual growing processes, because they permit each thing to follow its own natural course to the point of realization. The creation of the Myriad Things does not involve intentionality or purpose. The workings of the Tao are spontaneous.

The Zen monk Hanshan Deqing (1546–1623) describes the Realm of No-Mind. As so often, Zen Buddhism and Taoism speak the same language.

> *The Myriad Worlds*
> *Are flowers in the sky,*
> *The Mind and Body*
> *Moonlight on the water.*

Once Cunning
Ceases
And there are no more facts,
There is no place
For Thought.

THE MOTHER

All-under-Heaven
Has a Beginning,
A Mother.
To Attain the Mother,
Know the Children.
To Return Home
Cleave to the Mother,
Be safe from Peril.
Close the Apertures,
Shut the Gate,
Suffer and toil no longer.
Open the Apertures,
Meddle,
And never be safe.
To see the Small
Is Illumination,
To Cleave to the Soft
Is Strength.
Use the Light,

Return Home
To Illumination,
To No-Harm.
This is to Practice
Constancy.

THE RIVER MASTER

The Beginning is the Tao, Mother of All-under-Heaven, of the Myriad Things. The Child Knows its Mother. She in turn Knows her Child.

When the Apertures
Are closed,
The Eyes see
Correctly.
The Gate is
The Mouth.
Let the Mouth not utter
Wrong Words.

MAGISTER LIU

Be One
With the Tao,
Cleave to the Mother
Of All-under-Heaven,
See the Small
For what it is,
Do not Meddle—
This is True Illumination.

Return to the Mother, forget Words, Nurture Breath-Energy. Breath-Energy passes in and out through the Mouth. Close the Mouth, forget Words, and

Spirit finds Peace. Close the Gate, and Breath-Energy finds Calm in Non-Action, without toil, and the Great Tao is Complete. But if the Mouth stays open, endless Words will come tumbling out, heated discussions of this and that, concerns with petty matters. This is to forsake the Root and to chase twigs, to abandon the True for the False.

Duyvendak: The Mother is the Undifferentiated State, the Beginning, the Children are the Myriad Things. This Chapter seems to suggest an early matriarchal society. By Cleaving to the Mother in Mystic Union and closing the Apertures, i.e., the senses (just as in Ancient China jade disks were placed on the orifices of a corpse to prevent corruption), the natural development of the body is achieved [you will suffer and toil no longer], untrammeled by influences that shorten life. But through Action and Meddling one wears oneself out.

The "crazy monk" Cold Mountain (eighth century) in his simple verses often mused on the "way there," on "making it," Returning Home to the Calm of Cold Mountain.

>*Men ask the way to Cold Mountain.*
>*Cold Mountain: there's no through trail.*
>*In summer, the ice doesn't melt,*
>*The rising sun blurs in swirling fog.*
>*How did I make it?*
>*My Heart-and-Mind is not the same as yours.*
>*If yours was like mine*
>*You'd get it and be right here.*

BRAZEN ROBBERY

If, with a scrap
Of True Knowledge,
I walk on the road
Of the Great Tao,
Deviations
Are all that I fear.
The Great Tao
Is a broad and level Highway,
Yet most prefer
Tracks and bypaths.
The court seems
Well tended,
But the fields
Are choked with weeds,
The granaries bare.
Fancy clothes and sharp swords
Are on show,
Gluttonous feasting and drinking,
Material things in excess.
This is Brazen Robbery,
This is not the Tao!

THE RIVER MASTER

Lao-tzu has in mind the Rulers of his time, who refused to walk on the broad road of the Great Tao, the Highway of Non-Action. The foolish Multitude prefer bypaths, they prefer to walk down winding tracks:

> Following Deviations,
> False Ideas
> Of Excellence.

They do not have enough while the Ruler has too much. That is Brazen Robbery. This is Lao-tzu's passionate cry of protest.

MAGISTER LIU

The illuminating scrap of True Knowledge comes from the Constant Practice of the Tao, from continuous Observation of the Outer Radiance, from Contemplation of the Inner Marvel. It comes from single-minded Self-Cultivation, as opposed to the haphazard pursuit of strange and outlandish ways of thinking and fancy ideas.

> The Court
> Of such pretenders as these,
> Their Abode of Spirit,
> May Seem
> Well decked out,
> But it is hollow,
> It has been abandoned.
> The fields
> Of their Heart-and-Mind
> Are choked with weeds,
> Its granaries
> Are bare.

Sense-Apertures stand
Wide open,
Inner Vision is
Dimmed,
Inner Truth
Injured.
This is not
Self-Cultivation,
But Pursuit
Of False Knowledge.
Such as these
Indulge in fine clothes,
They wear sharp swords,
Argue contentiously,
Enjoy extravagant banquets,
Eschew plain grain
For fashionable drugs.

They forget the Root, hoping to attain the Tao through random conceits. These are Robbers of the Tao, they are braggarts and thieves.

JM: Underlying this whole Chapter is the double sense of the word *Tao*: on the one hand, Ultimate Meaning, Logos; on the other, the Way, or Road, the Highway. Robbers use fancy words and glib ideas to cloak brazen materialism, hollow deception, and exploitation of their fellow men. Lao-tzu advocates a simpler, more modest and devotional Tao.

Ursula K. Le Guin: So much for capitalism . . .

Cold Mountain:

Once at Cold Mountain
Troubles cease,
No more tangled

Hung-up mind.
Idly I scribble poems
On the rock cliff,
Taking whatever comes
Like a drifting boat.

WELL PLANTED, WELL EMBRACED

A shrub well planted
Is not easily uprooted,
A firm Embrace
Is not easily shaken off.
Descendants perpetuate
Ancestral sacrifices
Without intermission.
Cultivate the Person,
And Inner Power is True.
Cultivate the Family,
And Power Expands.
Cultivate the District,
And Power Endures.
Cultivate the Nation,
And Power Abounds.
Cultivate All-under-Heaven,

And Power is Universal.
Cultivation of the Person
Extends from Person to Family,
From Family to Nation,
To All-under-Heaven.
How do I know it
To be True?
From this,
From the Tao.

THE RIVER MASTER

When the Tao is firmly planted within the Person or the Nation, it cannot be uprooted. When the Spirit firmly Embraces the Tao, that Embrace is sure, it cannot be shaken off. When Self-Cultivation is Practiced within the Family, when the father is kind and the son filial, the elder brother is friendly and the younger obedient, the husband is sincere and the wife chaste,

This Inner Power
Creates a Bounty
Of Happiness
Extending
To future generations.

When the Tao is cultivated within a District, when the young behave respectfully toward their elders, when the young are themselves loved and nurtured, and the foolish and ignorant educated, then Inner Power protects all, shelters all. When the Tao is Cultivated within a Nation, and the Ruler is sincere,

Then the Inner Power
Extends
Abundantly,
Subjects are loyal,

True Benevolence and Justice
Flourish
Of-Themselves.

When the Highest Ruler Cultivates the Tao, the Inner Power is Universal throughout All-under-Heaven.

Without Words
All is
Transformed,
Without teaching
All is
Well Ruled.
The folk
Resonate with their Ruler
Like shadow or echo.

MAGISTER LIU

A plant that has mere Form and no Substance can easily be uprooted. A superficial Embrace that only has Form can easily be shaken off. But the Taoist's planting of Inner Power is a shrub well planted, it is a firm Embrace. It is Accomplished by Self-Cultivation, by rejection of all that is False.

The Taoist
Embraces the One
Through Non-Action.
This is the Marvel
That has no Form,
That leaves no tangible trace.
This Embrace
Can never be loosened.
This is
The Supreme
Planting,

The Supreme
Embrace.

Wayne W. Dyer: In this verse you're invited to see your role in the transformation of the planet. You do make a difference. You potentially have an infinite effect on the universe, you radiate Tao consciousness. You are like a wave of energy that illuminates a room—everyone will see the light and become affected.

Margaret Mead (quoted by Dyer): Never doubt that a small group of thoughtful, committed citizens can change the world. Indeed, it's the only thing that ever has.

Zhongchang Tong (179–220) testifies to the Inner Power of Self-Cultivation and Meditation, which extends through All-under-Heaven and "reaches the utmost limits of the Firmament."

Spirit attains Calm in the inner apartments, meditating on the Mysterious Void of Lao-tzu, Harmonizing Vital Essence by practicing breathing exercises. With one or two fellow initiates, the Tao is discussed, books explained. The Twin Powers of Yin and Yang, of Heaven and Earth, are examined, men and things are analyzed and explored. The strings of the Lute vibrate with the sublime melody of "The Southern Wind," a wondrous tune in a pure mode. In these free transports all worldly affairs are transcended, the space between Heaven and Earth is contemplated from on high. Topical demands of the times are left unheeded, Life and Life-Destiny are prolonged for ever. In this way one reaches the utmost limits of the Firmament, one emerges into a region beyond space and time.

THE INNER POWER OF THE INFANT

Abundant Inner Power
Is like an Infant,
Whom poisonous insects
Do not sting,
Whom fierce beasts
Do not seize,
Whom birds of prey
Do not attack.
The Infant's bones and sinews
Are Soft,
But its grasp
Is Sure.
The Infant knows nothing
Of the joining
Of Woman and Man,
And yet its member

Can stand erect,
Its Essence is Perfect.
All day
The Infant may cry,
But is never hoarse.
Its Harmony
Is Perfect.
To Know Harmony
Is Constancy,
To Know Constancy
Is Illumination.
To strive to Increase Life
Is Ill-omened,
Forces Heart-and-Mind
To consume Breath-Energy
Needlessly.
Things reach their prime,
They age Naturally.
To go against this
Is contrary to the Tao.
That which is contrary to the Tao
Will Perish all too soon.

THE RIVER MASTER

Whosoever Embraces the Tao firmly and contains within Self an Abundance of Inner Power is like an Infant. Spirit Light protects those who contain this Inner Power within, just as parents protect an Infant. The Infant does no Harm to other creatures, and so is not Harmed by them. The Infant's grasp is firm because its Heart-and-Mind is wholly concentrated. The Infant's member can stand erect, because it has within an Intact Abundance of Seminal Essence. It can cry from morning to night, but is never hoarse, because of its Perfect Inner Harmony. With Softness and Gentle Harmony there is Constancy in the Tao, there is Clarity and Calm. Breath-Energy grows daily stronger. But with the advent of Force, Harmonious Energy dwindles from within. Bodily Form is gradually further and further removed from the Tao, grows harder, more rigid, and Perishes prematurely.

MAGISTER LIU

This is the Abundant Primal Power of the Infant.

> Before its very first smile,
> At the very Beginning of Life,
> The Infant is
> Pure and naked,
> Undefiled,
> Knows neither Father nor Mother,
> Knows neither Self nor Other,
> Neither Inner nor Outer.

Gradually the Infant learns to smile, to hear and see like a Child, with a new awareness, while still Embracing the Truth.

> From within the Void,
> The Growing Child
> Begins to see
> White clouds and mist.

This Chapter speaks of the Infant, not the Child. The Infant's Spirit, its Breath-Energy, its Essence, are Pure and True. It is Empty and without Image, there is no Me, no Person, nothing to Harm. It is Complete and Perfect within. Nothing external can Harm it.

> Its penis may be aroused,
> May stand erect.
> This is the unstoppable
> Potency of the Infant,
> Its Perfect Essence.
> Its member is
> Marvelously in tune
> With the Tao.

The Primal Energy of the Infant is pure and intact, its crying issues forth from no Heart-and-Mind, from a Perfect Balance of Yin and Yang, from an intact Primal Essence. It is never hoarse.

Waley: The Emotions were thought by the Chinese to call upon and use up the original supply of Breath [Breath-Energy] which was allotted to a man at birth and constituted his life-spirit. Mencius, in whose system Conscience, sensitiveness to right and wrong, replaces the notion of the Tao, believed that the "morally great man" was one who had kept through later years his "Infant Heart."

Roger Ames and David Hall: The newly born Infant is an image of the fullness of potency, a robustness that makes it immune from environing evils . . . What gives the baby its vigor is its capacity to resound from the center, being supple yet firm, flexible yet potent. The baby, unconsciously and without motivation, is the embodiment of harmony and equilibrium. To try either to add to or to overspend this vitality is to introduce an element of coercion into the life process that produces the opposite effect. Persons still young can quickly become old and dry when they exhaust their resources by straining against the world.

Le Guin: As a metaphor of the Tao, the baby embodies the eternal beginning, the ever-springing source. "We come, trailing clouds of glory," Wordsworth says; and Hopkins, "There lives the dearest freshness deep down things." . . . We rise, flourish, fail. The Way never fails. We are waves. It is the sea.

Ruan Ji, Taoist poet and whistler of the Bamboo Grove, like Liu Ling, emulated the Naked Purity of the Infant.

> Ruan Ji was a man given to wine and uninhibited in all his actions. He would bare his head, let loose his hair, and sit naked with his legs spread out. Later idle aristocrats regarded him as their spiritual ancestor and claimed to have obtained the Root of the Great Tao. They threw away their bonnets, took off their clothes, and exhibited their nakedness like any animal.

MYSTIC UNION

Who Knows
Does not speak;
Who speaks
Does not Know.
Close the Mouth,
Shut the Gate.
Soften the Sharp,
Unravel the Tangles.
Harmonize the Light,
Blend with the Dust.
This is the Mystic Union.
Whosoever Attains this
Is neither loved
Nor rejected,
Receives neither Benefit
Nor Harm,
Is neither highly Esteemed
Nor Despised,
But is nonetheless
Greatly Valued
By All-under-Heaven.

THE RIVER MASTER

One who Knows
Values Deeds,
Not Words.
A chariot
Drawn by four fast horses
Is no match
For the galloping tongue
Of a fast talker.
Many Words bring
Much Sorrow.
Keep
The Apertures of Sense
Closed.

If a trace of hatred or bitterness still remains, unravel the Tangles with gentle thoughts of the Tao and of Non-Action.

Keep the Light of the Tao
Dark,
Do not let it
Shine.
Be One
With the Dust of the World,
Blend with it,
Do not stay aloof.
This is
The Mystic Union,
Of Heaven-and-Nature,
To be One
With the Tao.
Not to be
Loved,
Not to bask
In glory,
Not to suffer
From loneliness,
Not to be rejected,

> To feel no bitterness,
> But to have a Heart-and-Mind
> Of Calm and Constancy,
> With neither Desire nor Aversion.

For the Taoist, there is no Contending, no striving to be Master of the World, no bowing down to a benighted Ruler. There is neither Disgrace nor Pride, there is no Bitterness from unfulfilled ambition.

MAGISTER LIU

This Mystic Union is Union in the midst of Mystery, with no external Form or Trace, but with True Guidance from within. Love and Rejection, Benefit and Harm, Esteem and Disdain, these are all kept at a distance. The Inner Power of the Infant values Deeds over Knowledge and Words. Empty talk is no better than ignorance, no better than no Knowledge at all. The Mystic Union Embraces difference and sameness in the One. This is the Ultimate Mystery.

Le Guin: This is a Deep Sameness.

Duyvendak: All differences, all "oppositions," are annihilated in the Tao.

The Neo-Confucian philosopher Cheng Hao (1032–1085) wrote a poem on the wall of the temple where he was lodging while traveling the waterways of China. He speaks of the Calm Indifference, the freedom from Emotion, the Mystic Union, of the Man of the Tao. The fading of blossoms in autumn is part of Nature. The Taoist does not allow Emotion to color such perceptions.

> *Going north,*
> *Heading south,*
> *Stopping wherever possible,*
> *Seeing the duckweed bloom*
> *Then fade*

In autumn
Across the rivers of the Southland.
The Man of the Tao
On his travels
Never grieves
For autumn,
But lets the evening hills
Themselves
Quietly share their sorrow.

OF THEIR OWN ACCORD

"Rule a Nation
With the Judgment
Of Righteousness,
Wage War
With Cunning."
To this the Taoist replies,
"Win All-under-Heaven
Through Not-Meddling."
How do I know it
To be True?
Through this,
Through the Tao.
With more Restrictions
And Prohibitions
In All-under-Heaven,
The folk are the poorer.
The more Sharp Weapons
Are wielded,
The more benighted
Is the Nation.
With Cunning Skills,

Strange Contraptions
And Devices
Proliferate.
With Laws and Decrees,
There are more
Robbers and thieves.
So the Taoist says:
"I Return
To Non-Action,
And the folk are Transformed
Of their own accord,
Of-Themselves.
I Cherish Calm,
And they are set right
Of-Themselves.
I do not Meddle,
And they prosper
Of their own accord.
I am free of Desire
And they Return
To the Uncarved Block
Of their own accord."

THE RIVER MASTER

With Not-Meddling
And Non-Action
All-under-Heaven is won.
This Truth I know
From the Tao
In the present Moment.

A host of Prohibitions only makes the folk ever more deceitful. They do each other Harm, and the end result is increased poverty and misery. As Cunning Skills proliferate, such as elaborate decoration, the building of intricate palaces, the carving and cutting of precious stones, and the making of fine raiment, the folk will covet the gorgeous gold and jade inlays, the richly colored artifacts possessed by their superiors. The more highly developed the connoisseurship of such beautiful objects, the more the farming of the land and other such Simple Activities are neglected, the more hunger and cold become rampant, the more robbers and thieves prey on the unfortunate. So the Taoist says:

> I change nothing,
> And the folk are
> Transformed and Perfected.
> I do not Meddle,
> And they prosper
> Of-Themselves.
> I love Calm,
> And they are
> Loyal and law-abiding
> Of-Themselves.
> I am free of Desire,
> And they are Simple
> Of-Themselves,
> Simple as
> The Uncarved Block.

MAGISTER LIU

With Not-Meddling, the folk enjoy Simple Well-Being. There are no strange devices, no robbers and thieves. The Taoist dwells in Non-Action, and the folk are Transformed in accordance with the So-of-Itself. Non-Being transforms Being. The Taoist's Not-Meddling brings prosperity, it nourishes Energy. The Tao of the Mystic Union is simply the Tao of Not-Meddling. Person and Nation can either be Ruled Forcefully, as with a Weapon, or Gently, as in the Tao. Judgment and Cunning are both of them forms of

Meddling, forms of Force, as opposed to the So-of-Itself, the Natural Flow of the Tao. All-under-Heaven surrenders willingly to the Gentle Art of the Tao. In the individual Person, forceful prohibitions merely lead to a Decay of Spirit. The Taoist's freedom from Desire guides the folk to turn inward to the Uncarved Block.

> They Return Home
> To the Root.
> This is
> The Great Setting-to-Right
> Of No-Setting-to-Right,
> The Great Tactic
> Of No-Tactic.
> All is Accomplished
> Through Non-Action.
> The Heart-and-Mind
> Is at Peace.
> There are no Cares
> In All-under-Heaven.

JM: Much of this is a Taoist response to the cynical ideas set out in Sun-tzu's *The Art of War*, and to the draconian ideology of the Legalists, China's first fascists.

Chen: Lao-tzu's ideal of Non-Action can be seen both as a remedy to dissolve the tyrannical inclinations of those in power, and as a stimulant to encourage the self-expression of the folk. If the people of the world who control the reins of political power were all able to Return to Non-Action, to Cherish Calm, and not to Meddle, to be Free of Desire, then peace for mankind would be within our grasp.

Ruan Ji wrote eloquently of the virtues of No-Rule.

> In days of old, men followed their Fate, and preserved them-
> selves with moderation. The bright did not conquer because of their

Knowledge. The ignorant were not crushed because of their stupidity. The weak were not cowed by oppression, nor did the strong Prevail by Force. In those days of old, there was no Ruler, and all beings were at Peace. There were no Officials, and affairs were well ordered.

THE UNSHINING TAOIST

When the Ruler
Is Dull,
The folk
Are Happy.
When the Ruler
Is Busy and Alert,
They are Discontented.
Fortune and Calamity
Are part of each other,
Calamity
Is Latent within Fortune.
How few
Recognize that Margin
Where there is
No Judgment of Right?
Right

Can become Cunning,
Good
Can become Evil,
And mankind
Is long gone astray.
The Taoist is
Square but not cut-square,
Has corners
That are not pointed,
Is straight
But not taut.
The Light of the Taoist
Does not shine.

THE RIVER MASTER

The Taoist Ruler teaches his subjects to be Generous. This Teaching may seem Dull, it may seem to lack Light.

But the folk
Are Happy,
They prosper,
They live in friendship.

But when the Ruler is alert and busy, then the folk:

Speak with their Mouths,
Not from their Hearts.
Words reach no further
Than their Ears,
Deeper Trust and Understanding
Are lost.
The Taoist is straight,
But bends

To Follow others,
Without displaying Self.
The Taoist glows,
Does not shine.

MAGISTER LIU

The Greater Right of No-Right, of No-Judgment, Prevails over the Ordinary Right of Judgment. It may seem Dull, whereas Ordinary Right appears sharp and alert.

Non-Action,
Not-Meddling,
No-Heart-and-Mind,
Clarity and Calm,
Bring All-under-Heaven
To the Greater Right.

There is no narrow Judgment of Right in the Taoist Ruler's Heart-and-Mind. The folk are Transformed Of-Themselves by the Ruler's Breath-Energy, they are Happy and Contented. But when the Ruler is busy Meddling, then a narrow sense of Right is entrenched in the Heart-and-Mind, and the Cycle of Fortune and Calamity commences.

The Taoist
Glows
With a Contained Light,
With the Dark Light
Of Spirit.
This is
The Greater Right
Stemming from a Root
Deep in the Tao.

Waley: For the Taoist the real "Bourn" of Wisdom, the Margin, lies far beyond the world of contraries and antinomies.

Bo Juyi describes his sense of Calm and Release, upon reading *The Book of Taoist Master Zhuang*.

Far from home,
Parted from kin,
Banished to a strange place,
I wonder that my heart feels
So little anguish
So little pain.
Reading Master Zhuang,
I have discovered
My True Home,
In Nothing-Land.

THRIFT

In Ruling Others,
In serving
Heaven-and-Nature,
Nothing excels
Thrift.
Early Surrender
To the Tao
Brings a Double Measure
Of Inner Power,
A Power that
Prevails over all,
A Power that
Has no bounds,
That can
Possess a Nation.
Possessing
The Mother of the Nation,
It Endures.
It has a Deep Root

And a Firm Stalk.
This is the Tao of Long Life,
Of Enduring Vision.

THE RIVER MASTER

Thrift is a Love that cares for every smallest detail. A Ruler who loves the folk
and cares for their prosperity should not countenance extravagance:

Should care for every detail,
Let nothing casually
Fall away.
The Deep Root
Is Breath-Energy,
The Firm Stalk
Is Spirit Essence.

MAGISTER LIU

Thrift is the careful harvesting of Breath-Energy and Spirit Essence, a
Wise Economy of Heart-and-Mind, one that does not set undue store by
superficial Talent and Ability. To surrender to the Tao of Thrift is to
gather a Double Measure of Inner Power. With this, all selfish Desire is
eliminated.

The Mother is
Close at hand,
Life Endures
In an unceasing Flow.

Thrift is a small word for a large idea. It is the key to Ruling Others and serving Heaven-and-Nature. To Rule Others with Thrift, one must Observe the
Outer Radiance with Desire, one must Contemplate the Inner Marvel free

from Desire. Gradually the Human Heart-and-Mind is extinguished. To
serve Heaven-and-Nature with Thrift:

> Contemplate
> The Inner Marvel
> Free from Desire,
> Keep Simple Undyed Silk
> In view,
> Embrace the Uncarved Block,
> Return
> To Heaven-and-Nature.

This is not lightly Achieved, it is the result of daily Practice in the Tao, of
cherishing Breath-Energy, of not letting it drain away. This brings a Double
Measure of Inner Power. Desire is extinguished and the True Principle of
Heaven-and-Nature comes forth unsullied. The Nation is not out there some-
where, it is within, it is the most excellent Terrain of Heart-and-Mind. The
Seeker of the Tao,

> Puts all
> Meddling and Business
> Aside,
> Returns
> To the True Elixir,
> Abides
> In that Highest Terrain.
> This is the True Seed.
> The Son Returns to the Mother,
> Cleaves to her.
> The Son knows the Man,
> But Cleaves to the Woman.
> The Son is Nourished
> By the Mother,
> Builds strength
> From softest shoots,
> From tiniest details.

Chen: Lao-tzu, in proposing the concept of Thrift, is not only speaking of material things. In fact, his emphasis is on the spiritual aspects of Life. Thrift is the Cultivation of Inner Strength, the consolidation of one's natural genuineness and the fulfillment of one's natural potential. It is expending one's energies in the proper area without wasting them on external attachment.

Waley: The Double Measure of one's stock of Breath-Energy, of Inner Power, is Attained by Quietist Practices, by Spiritual Thrift.

Ames and Hall: Thrift is Husbandry of Vital Energy, Nourishing the Life-Force through Self-Cultivation, expending creative energies judiciously. This personal regimen also prepares one to create a Vision for the Human Community.

The eccentric painter Zhu Da, known as Bada Shanren (ca. 1626–1705), compared the Cultivation of the Tao to a massive draft of river water!

> *Not-One*
> *Cannot be divided.*
> *Not-Two*
> *Doesn't have Two Names.*
> *Drink West River*
> *To the dregs—*
> *That might tell you something*
> *About the Tao!*

COOKING A SMALL FISH

Ruling a Great Nation
Is like
Cooking a Small Fish.
When All-under-Heaven
Is Ruled by the Tao,
Demons lose
Their Spirit Power.
What Power they have
Can do no Harm.
The Taoist Ruler
Does no Harm.
Inner Powers combine
To Return Home
To the Tao.

THE RIVER MASTER

In the cooking of a small fish, the innards should not be removed, the scales should not be scraped off. Do not handle a small fish too much, in case it disintegrates. If Rulers Meddle, the folk are distressed. Similarly, if Self-Cultivation (the Ruling of the Person) entails unnecessary Business, Inner Essence dissipates.

> When All-under-Heaven
> Is Ruled
> With the Tao and the Power,
> Demons cannot cause Harm,
> They cannot Harm
> Purity,
> Nature,
> The So-of-Itself.

The Taoist Ruler, his subjects, and the Spirits at large in All-under-Heaven can thus enjoy a shared Inner Power.

> They all Return Home
> To the Tao.

MAGISTER LIU

When All-under-Heaven is Ruled by the Tao, when the Tao of the So-of-Itself Rules, then Demons cease to exercise Malign Spirit Power, they become No-Spirit, Ultimate Spirit, they are One with the Tao of the So-of-Itself and of Non-Action.

> To Rule a Nation
> In the manner of
> Cooking a Small Fish
> Is Non-Action.
> The Tao of Thrift
> And Enduring Vision

Is not Large,
It is One,
Not Two,
It is Dark,
It does not shine.

The Large is Hard and Forceful, the Small is Soft and Gentle. To Rule a Great Nation in the manner of cooking a Small Fish is to use the Soft and Gentle to pacify the Hard and Forceful.

Mathieu: This Chapter is all about subtlety and a light touch in politics (*délicatesse et distanciation par rapport à la chose politique*), just as cooking a Small Fish is all about quick frying (*la petite friture*) as opposed to boiling (*cuisson à l'eau*). The Demons are malign influences whose ability to Harm is rendered impotent, is neutralized, by the Taoist Inner Power of the Ruler.

Chen: If the government is able to implement Non-Action and bring about a state of Calm and social stability, then there is no external force [no Spirit] which can do them injury and the folk will be free to follow their natural course and live peacefully.

The poet and mountaineer Xie Lingyun describes his Taoist quest for Simplicity.

*On these hills
I shake the Dust of the World
From my clothes,
And stroll
Into my tumbleweed house . . .
Spring and my Heart
Have now become One . . .
Joy and Sorrow
Come and go in turn.
Now failure*

Daunts us,
Now success
Makes us glad.
I'd rather be free for ever,
I choose Simplicity,
The Uncarved Block.

DOWNSTREAM

A Great Nation
Is Downstream,
It is Woman
In the Union
Of All-under-Heaven.
Woman Prevails
Over Man
Through her Calm.
In Calm
She lies Beneath.
Likewise
A Great Nation
Gets beneath
A Small Nation,
And wins its Allegiance.
A Small Nation
Is beneath
A Great Nation,
And gives Allegiance.
Some get beneath,
Others *are* beneath,
Each attains its wishes.

A Great Nation
Seeks to gather Others
And Nourish them.
A Small Nation seeks
To Serve the Other.
The Great
Should place itself
Beneath.

THE RIVER MASTER

Woman is Yin,
Humble, Soft,
And Harmonious.
Woman is not preeminent,
But nonetheless
Subdues Man.
Yin Prevails over Yang,
Through being Calm,
Being Gentle,
Through not seeking Domination.
The Tao of Yin is
One of Calm and Humility.

MAGISTER LIU

In Calm
She lies Beneath.
This Union
Of Woman and Man
Is the very Foundation

Of Life-Destiny.
The Great is Yang,
Man, Hard.
The Small is Yin,
Woman, Soft.
Woman Prevails Beneath
Through Calm,
Prevails over Hard,
Over Man,
Through Softness.
When Man unites
With Woman,
Hard submits
To Soft.
Woman's Calm
Prevails over Man,
Hard is contained
Within Soft.

The twin Energies of Man and Woman merge into One, they find Nourishment in this Marvelous Union of Yin and Yang, Man Cleaving Gently to Woman. Whosoever knows only how to be Man and not Woman, whosoever knows only the Great and not the Small, knows only Movement and not Calm, in such a one neither Yin nor Yang can thrive. Calm kindles Movement, Movement is rooted in Calm, Calm and Movement are One Being.

Waley: For the woman to get underneath is to induce the man to mount her.

JM: This Chapter hails the cosmic significance of sexual intercourse, and the importance of the Yin, the Soft, the Gentle, the Woman, in the Taoist scheme of things. (Li Ling agrees, quoting at length from a fragment of a lost Taoist alchemical text.) This is how Bo Xingjian (776–827), brother of the poet Bo Juyi, entitles his erotic Rhapsody: "The Great Joy of the Union of Heaven and Earth, of Yin and Yang."

Wilhelm: To keep oneself Downstream is to keep oneself free from Pretense, to hold back, to exercise Restraint. The Great Nation by its Restraint motivates the Small Nation to affiliate itself. The Small Nation profits from the affiliation and is assured of Protection against enemy Aggression.

Jiang Yan (444–505) sings of the Taoist Union with Nature.

> *When the Great Simplicity*
> *First divided,*
> *It quickened the Myriad Forms*
> *Into Being . . .*
> *All Returns to the One.*
> *In Attaining the Tao*
> *We touch only*
> *The Change*
> *That moves through all,*
> *The Fire*
> *That burns its way through Kindling.*
> *Strive to purify*
> *Innermost Heart-and-Mind,*
> *Be rid of*
> *Artifice and Guile.*
> *When Self and Others*
> *Are both forgotten,*
> *Then the seagulls*
> *Are our friends.*

The Taoist Master Lie (Lieh-tzu) had written:

> There was a man who lived by the sea and loved seagulls. Every day at dawn when he went down to the sea to swim, the gulls followed him. This was a sign that he was completely in tune with Nature.

THE INNER SANCTUARY

The Tao
Is the Inner Sanctuary
Of the Myriad Things,
Treasure
Of the Good,
Refuge
Of the Not-so-Good.
Fine Words
May purchase
High Regard,
Fine Deeds
May win
Esteem
Even for
Doers of evil.
The Not-so-Good
Are never rejected.

When the Son of Heaven
Was enthroned,
And the Three Dukes
Enfeoffed,
They were presented
With fine jades,
Racing steeds
Pranced before them.
Would it not have been
Better by far
For them to sit still
And enter the Tao?
Why was the Tao
So highly Esteemed
Of Old?
Was it not said
That by seeking it,
By Attaining it,
One escaped
The consequences of one's errors?
For this the Tao was Esteemed
By All-under-Heaven.

THE RIVER MASTER

The Inner Sanctuary of the Tao contains everything. It is the Treasure of the Good, but also protects the Not-so-Good, the Imperfect. They too can rely on it. Through Remorse and Humility, they are Transformed in the Tao. In ancient times they were never rejected.

The Inner Power
Transformed them,

It made them
Pure.
The Three Dukes
Were well advised
To sit still
And enter the Tao.

MAGISTER LIU

This Inner Sanctuary of the Tao is Supremely Great, there is nothing that is not contained in it, no Principle of Truth it does not Embrace. The Son of Heaven and the Three Dukes should enter it, and sit still.

The Tao is
Primal Mother
Of the Myriad Things,
Ancestral Lord
Of the Myriad Things,
Their Sanctuary.
The grain
Contained in the Sanctuary
Is the Nourishment
Of Outer Radiance.

Even the Not-so-Good can come to Know this Sanctuary, and are never rejected for their Imperfections. In Attaining the Tao they are carried to the Other Shore, they escape the errors of their ways.

Ames and Hall: The Tao is a healer, a source of hope for those who have strayed, it is forgiving.

JM: The Inner Sanctuary (*ao*) is traditionally explained as the southwest corner of the house, where the wife slept with the Master beside her. It was a place of Yin fecundity, offering protection to the house from its dark recesses, just as the Tao Embraces and Nourishes All-under-Heaven.

Xie Lingyun describes his sudden awareness of the Tao in the mountains.

My path winds round
A curving river,
To climb far
Among rocky crags . . .
When I survey
All this,
The world of men
Disappears,
In a flash of enlightenment
Everything
Falls away.

BUSY ABOUT NO-BUSINESS

Accomplish
Through Non-Action,
Be Busy
About No-Business,
Taste
No-Taste.
Consider
The Great
Small,
The Many
Few.
Requite Bitterness
With Inner Power,
See the Difficult
In the Easy,
The Great
In the Small.
In All-under-Heaven

Deal with the Difficult
While it's Easy,
Deal with the Great
In the Smallest Detail.
The Taoist never
Deals with Greatness,
And so
Achieves Greatness.
A promise lightly made
Is not to be believed.
Things considered Easy
Are often Difficult.
The True Taoist
Conceives Difficulty,
And so
Encounters none.

THE RIVER MASTER

With Non-Action, everything is Accomplished.

Taste No-Taste,
Taste
The True Meaning
Of the Tao.
Seek to turn
The Large
Into the Small,
The Many
Into the Few.

Put an end to Misfortune while it is still unborn. Embark upon Difficulties while they are still Easy, before they mature. Remember that Calamity and Chaos arise out of small details.

MAGISTER LIU

Seen in the Light of the Enduring, nothing is Difficult. Every Difficulty in All-under-Heaven arises from something Easy. Everything Great in All-under-Heaven arises from some Small Detail. A great deal of human error arises from Excessive Action in dealing with the Great and the Difficult, forsaking the close at hand in search of something distant. By not thinking of the Great as Great, one can Attain True Greatness. The Taoist sets out from a lowly station in order to reach the heights, sets out from a place close at hand in order to reach the distance. The Taoist Accomplishes through Non-Action, the So-of-Itself, the Way of Nature, is Busy about No-Business, tastes No-Taste with the dispassionate appreciation of the Connoisseur, with Clarity and Calm. These are the Lodging and Home of the Tao, they are the Outer Radiance and the Inner Marvel. With these, every Difficulty can be dealt with, however Great it may seem.

Duyvendak: Non-Action is to force nothing, always to keep an eye open for that phase in its development in which a thing is still weak and quiet. That is the point where one should take it up.

Chen: To "conceive Difficulty" is the attitude of an attentive and serious person—being prudent with confidences, circumspect in thought, and conscientious in conduct.

In his portrait of "The Man of the Tao," Xie Lingyun describes the world of the True Taoist, both a physical dwelling and an Inner Realm.

> The Supreme Man is above all Desire for Fame. He enters the Tao and takes up his abode in Truth. He lets his Intelligence lie fallow and his Knowledge diminish. He withdraws himself bodily and flees from Self. He builds himself a house high in the hills, far removed, a mysterious dwelling of utmost Emptiness, hung round with wild

plants like a mist. Water runs around it this way and that, dashing against the rocks. The sun peers through the clouds from time to time. Drifting blossoms fall brightly into the stream across the way, while the enshrouding mists loom like mountain peaks. He discovers the principles of Heaven and Earth from within his own solitary Being. He straddles the four seas within the compass of his Heart-and-Mind. He leaps beyond the Dust of the World and sees things as they are.

SUCHNESS, THE SO-OF-ITSELF

That which is
At Peace
Is easily maintained,
That which has given
No Sign
Is easily dealt with.
Brittle things
Are easily broken,
Fine things
Easily dispersed.
Act
Before there is Substance,
Create Order

Before Chaos gets under way.

A stout tree

An arm's span in girth

Grew from

A tiny shoot.

A mighty terrace

Nine stories high

Began as

A mound of earth.

A journey

Of a thousand leagues

Commenced with

A single step.

Action

Invites Failure.

Whosoever Grips

Loses.

The Taoist never Acts

And never Fails,

Never Grips

And never Loses.

The folk often Fail

On the verge

Of Completion.

Heed Conclusion

No less than Commencement,

And there is

No Failure.

The Taoist Desires No-Desire,

Does not value

Goods that are

Hard to come by,

Studies No-Study,
Returns to that which
The Multitude leave behind,
Refrain from Action,
Nourish the Myriad Things
In their Suchness,
The So-of-Itself.

THE RIVER MASTER

When there is Peace, while the seeds of Misfortune have not yet sprouted, and the fruits of Desire have not yet ripened and become tangible, while Misfortune is still weak and easily broken, while it is still fine and easily dispersed, then it is not hard to practice Self-Cultivation and to Rule a Nation. This is the relation of Being to Non-Being. When something is about to sprout from Non-Being, it must be prevented if at all possible from coming into Being. Rule the Nation through Self-Cultivation, before Chaos has arisen. Close the Gate beforehand. Proceed from the Small to the Great, from the Low to the High, from what is near to what is far away. Meddling spoils things, it goes against Nature, against the grain. The Taoist abides in Non-Action, spoils nothing, and meets with no Failure. The Multitude value Brilliance and Outward Show, but the Taoist values Buried Light, Hidden Splendor, Reality, and Simplicity. The Multitude study False Wisdom and Hypocrisy, the Taoist studies No-Study, Suchness, the So-of-Itself. The Multitude study how to Rule the World, the Taoist studies Self-Cultivation, how to Rule Self, how to preserve the True Wisdom of the Tao.

The Taoist Returns Home
To what Others
Leave behind.
Others forsake
The Root
For the Branch,
Forsake the Fruit
For the Flower.

The Taoist Returns
To the Root,
Helps all beings
To be Natural and Free.

MAGISTER LIU

If one abides in Non-Action, in Peace and Calm, if one never Grips, then problems that have as yet given no Sign are easy to deal with. But once Action and Gripping commence, even if a matter is near to Completion, it may still Fail. So the Taoist Eschews Action that goes beyond what is Natural, beyond Suchness, the So-of-Itself.

True Knowledge
Of the Inner Springs
Of All-under-Heaven
Is to be found
In the interstices between
Being
And Non-Being,
In those dark
Inchoate moments,
When Good and Evil
Are still indistinct,
When things
Have given no Sign
And are still
Easy to manipulate.
One who pays no heed
To Beginnings
Will surely Fail,
One who proceeds
Without examining
The Springs
Will Lose.
The Taoist

Contemplates
The Inner Marvel,
The Inner Springs
Before they have come
Into Being,
Studies No-Study,
Nourishes
The Suchness-of-Themselves
Of the Myriad Things.

The Taoist Observes the Outer Radiance as the Springs become visible. The Taoist's Heart-and-Mind is Transformed, and all the Myriad Things are Transformed, without Artifice or Effort.

They Return
To the So-of-Itself,
To Nature,
To Suchness.
The Seeker of the Tao
Is Relaxed,
Motionless,
Silent,
Resonant,
Connected to All-under-Heaven,
Free from the stirrings
Of the Human Heart-and-Mind.

Waley: The Multitude have abandoned the old Simple Ways, such things as walking instead of riding, using Knotted Ropes instead of writing.

Xie Lingyun draws a picture of the Taoist Recluse.

When the Recluse shows himself, he is like a Roving Dragon. When he retreats he is like a Hidden Phoenix. The Recluse comes from no one knows where, and goes to no one knows where . . . He is desolate when autumn comes but flourishes in the spring. He plays the Lute beneath the bright moon and pours himself wine in the gentle breeze. He travels far away, riding on the pure wind. He rides high in the air, brushing away the white clouds. If you ask where you might meet such a Recluse, the answer is "throughout the world." The Recluse fixes his gaze beyond worldly limits.

THE GRAND FLOW

Of Old
Taoists did not
Impart Illumination,
They kept the folk
Foolish.
Too much Wisdom
Makes them
Hard to Rule.
To Rule
Through Wisdom
Is to Rob the Nation!
To rule
Through absence of Wisdom
Is to Bless the Nation!
To understand
This True Pattern
Is to have
Mystic Power.
Mystic Power is
Deep,

It is
Distant,
It Returns with things
To their Source,
It Attains
The Grand Flow.

THE RIVER MASTER

The Ancients chose
Not to Illuminate
By the Tao
And Inner Power,
But instead
Taught the folk
How to remain Simple,
How not to become
Hypocrites.

Through a surfeit of so-called Knowledge and Wisdom, the folk become hard to rule, they become Cunning and Hypocritical. To Rule them by so-called Wisdom is therefore to Rob them, is to remove them from the Tao and the Inner Power.

To Rule a Nation
Without False Wisdom
Makes for Happiness.
Ruler and subjects
Are closer to one another,
King and minister
Work happily together.

True Wisdom and Pure Ignorance are a Pattern for the Practice of Self-Cultivation and for the Rule of the Nation.

To know this,
To abide by it,
This is Mystic Power.
A Turning,
A Return.

Mystic Power is Generous, wishing to bring Others to Completion. This is the
Grand Flow.

MAGISTER LIU

Mystic Power is Deep and Distant, it cannot be sought out, it cannot be Attained by so-called Wisdom.

It is reached
Through
Pure Folly,
Returning with things
To their Source,
To the Tao,
Following Gently
In the Grand Flow.
Others Cultivate
False Illumination
And Knowledge,
Causing them
To shine
More and more brightly,
Making them
Blaze and sparkle,
Claiming these to be
The Tao.
But this Brilliance
Belongs to
The Cycle of Life and Death.

The Taoists of Old did not seek Illumination by way of False Knowledge and
Cunning, but instead sought the Transformation that comes of Folly.

This brought
Clarity and Calm
To their thinking.
With Wisdom
Vain Thoughts
Populate the Heart-and-Mind.
Once so-called Wisdom
Has puffed them up,
These Thoughts are
Hard to bring to Order,
Hard to Rule.

The Heart-and-Mind is the Nation of the Person. To Rule this Inner Nation and its folk with False Wisdom is to Control Thought with Action, with alert intelligence. This does not bring Calm to thinking, it gives rise to further disorderly Thoughts, after which neither Person nor Nation can be at Peace. This is to Rob both Nation and Person of Calm. To Rule a Nation with the Tao is to be Calm, it is to stop Controlling things forcefully with the Human Heart-and-Mind, to let Natural Thoughts arise, Of-Themselves, in their Pure Suchness. This brings Calm to the Person, and Blessing to the Nation. This is Mystic Power, a Power too fine and subtle to be seen or heard.

Chen: What Lao-tzu means by "keeping the folk Foolish," is restoring them to their Original Nature, to Simple Calm and Sincerity, so that they Return to a state of mind unrestricted by prejudice and value judgments. Those who Rule should refrain from corrupting this genuineness and Natural Simplicity.

The Hermit Cold Mountain found Calm, sitting under the pine trees, listening to the gentle breeze.

I wanted a good place
To settle:
Cold Mountain
Seemed safe.
A light breeze
Blows in the quiet pines,

Listen closely
And it sounds even better.
Under the trees
A gray-haired man
Mumbles as he reads Lao-tzu.
For ten years
I've not gone Home,
I've forgotten
The way I came.

KINGS OF THE HUNDRED VALLEYS

River and Ocean are
Kings of the Hundred Valleys
Through being Beneath.
This is why
They are Kings.
Whosoever wishes to be
Above the folk,
In speech must be
Beneath them.
Whosoever wishes to be
Ahead of them
Must be
Behind.
The Taoist is Above,
And yet they feel
No Burden,
Is Ahead,
And they feel
No Impediment.

All-under-Heaven
Propels the Taoist forward
Joyfully,
Untiringly.
The Taoist Ruler
Never Contends
With Others,
All-under-Heaven
Never Contends
With the Taoist Ruler.

THE RIVER MASTER

River and Ocean lie Beneath, and all the currents of Water are drawn toward them. Just so the folk are drawn, they turn toward the Taoist Ruler, who is King of all the Valleys, who emulates River and Ocean and abides in a humble and lowly position. The Taoist loves the folk deeply like little children.

MAGISTER LIU

River and Ocean lie Beneath, they never Contend, and so they are Kings of every watercourse, of the Hundred Valleys. In the same way the Taoist Ruler is Beneath, he never Contends, and so is King of All-under-Heaven. The Mystic Power and the Grand Flow stem from a Generous Heart-and-Mind that knows no Contending, from a Heart-and-Mind of Emptiness. It takes in all things, and nothing suffers Harm.

From Beneath,
River and Ocean
Are Connected with all,
They are Empty,
Deep,

Distant,
They are Infinite.
All the Waters
Return Home to them.
They are
Kings of the Hundred Valleys.
They share
The Inner Power of Humility.

Chen: The Ruler, by Not-Contending, by setting an example for the folk, can assure himself of a stable government and society. The folk do not consider the Ruler to be a Burden, they are not oppressed, because everyone receives his proper share.

Li Bo wrote a short poem for his friend the Taoist Hermit Yuan Danqiu.

I envy you, my friend,
Dwelling on East Mountain,
Lover of beauteous hills and valleys,
Asleep in the green season of spring
Among empty forests,
Rising long after daybreak,
The wind in the pines
Blowing through your sleeves,
The stony brook washing your soul.
I envy you,
Lying there unperturbed,
Pillowed high
On your emerald mist!

THE THREE TREASURES

All-under-Heaven
Considers my Tao
Great,
And yet it Resembles
Nothing.
It Resembles
Nothing
Because it is
Great.
If it Resembled
Something,
It would be
Small.
I have Three Treasures
To Hold and to Cherish.
The first is
Compassion,
The second
Frugality,
The third
Self-Effacement,
Refusal to take precedence

Over All-under-Heaven.
With Compassion
Comes Courage.
With Frugality
Comes Generosity.
With Self-Effacement
Comes
The capacity to be
A Chief Instrument.
Courage
Without Compassion,
Generosity
Without Frugality,
Eminence
Without Self-Effacement,
These are Death!
With Compassion
Comes True Victory in Warfare,
And sure Protection.
Heaven saves,
Compassion protects.

THE RIVER MASTER

Compassion means:
I love the folk
Like little children.
Frugality means:
With every tax I raise
I feel I am
Parting with my own money.

Self-Effacement means:
I never wish to be a Leader
In All-under-Heaven.
I Cultivate
Modesty and Seclusion.

Now whosoever is Kind and Compassionate, such a one is truly Courageous, staunch in loyalty and filial devotion. Whosoever is Frugal is large-minded and Generous. When the Son of Heaven is Frugal and Generous, then the folk receive daily Benefit from his Generosity. Whosoever does not wish to play the Leader in All-under-Heaven, whosoever is Self-Effacing and has no Desire to be the Head of All-under-Heaven, such a one will be a Complete Vessel, a Chief Instrument. This is the True Taoist.

MAGISTER LIU

My Tao Resembles Nothing because it is Great beyond the bounds of Form and Image. The Three Treasures of Compassion, Frugality, and Self-Effacement truly Resemble Nothing. To cherish these Three "Like-Nothing" Treasures, and never to lose them, is to be genuinely Courageous and Generous, is to be a True Chief Instrument. Of the Three Treasures, the principal one is Compassion. Frugality and Self-Effacement derive from Compassion. With Compassion, if one Cleaves Firmly to the Tao, one will Prevail, even in Warfare. If I live a life of Compassion, Heaven-and-Nature will keep me Safe, will protect me. My Heart-and-Mind will be One with the Heart-and-Mind of Heaven-and-Nature, of the Tao. My Inner Power will be a worthy partner for Heaven. If the Great Tao were to Resemble Something, if it had a recognizable Form and Image, then it would be something petty and cunning, it would be some trifling ability, which would never amount to anything truly Great. The Three Treasures are Attained through Self-Cultivation, through Observation of the Outer Radiance and Contemplation of the Inner Marvel. They must be Cherished, and never lost. Compassion makes no distinction between Me and Other. This is True Courage, the Courage of True Compassion. Frugality is Clarity and Calm, No-Desire, bathed in the Light of the Tao, in the Myriad Principles of Truth, new every day. The Frugal Person is filled with Inner Power, with Generosity. Self-Effacement is Being that Resembles Non-Being, it is Substance that resembles Void. The more lowly the Heart-and-Mind, the higher the Tao. Courage, Generosity, and Being-the-Chief-Instrument Resemble Nothing, but they are Great. Their Greatness lies in Resembling Nothing. All Three are a necessary Foundation for the conduct of the Person, for dealing with the World. Cleave to them all, in their Seeming Nothingness, and thus enter the Terrain of Life.

Waley: These are the three rules that formed the practical, political side of the author's teaching: (1) [pity, compassion] abstention from aggressive war and capital punishment, (2) [frugality, thrift] absolute simplicity of living, (3) [refusal to be foremost of all things under heaven] refusal to assert active authority. [Heaven keeps safe, Compassion protects.] Heaven arms with pity those whom it would not see destroyed.

Li Bo yearns for the peace and freedom of the mountains.

> *O mountains of renown*
> *That I adore!*
> *You fill my heart*
> *With deep repose.*
> *I may drink many*
> *Precious potions,*
> *But still I must needs wash*
> *The Dust from my face.*
> *Let me abide*
> *With the things I love,*
> *Let me leave the world of man*
> *For ever.*

THE POWER OF NOT-CONTENDING

The best Soldier

Is not Warlike.

The best Warrior

Never fights

Out of Wrath.

The best Victory

Does not Engage the Enemy.

The best Deployment of Others

Is from Beneath.

This is the Power

Of Not-Contending,

This is Strength

In the deployment of Others,

This is to be

A Worthy Companion

Of Heaven-and-Nature,

Of the Supreme Tao
Of Old.

THE RIVER MASTER

A Warrior of the Tao
Deflects Misfortune
Before it sprouts
Into Wrath.
A Warrior of the Tao
Prevails
Without doing battle.
The Enemy submits
Of its own accord.

This is the Inner Power of Not-Contending.

MAGISTER LIU

The Worthy Companion
Of Heaven-and-Nature
Cleaves to the Tao
Of the So-of-Itself,
Of Nature,
Of Non-Action,
Of Not-Contending.

Victory does not necessarily go to the Aggressor. The best Army has no Heart-and-Mind for battle, it never engages out of Wrath. The True Victor fears Defeat, Retreats, does not Advance, does not engage.

This is War
Without the Heart-and-Mind

Of War,
With no Trace
Of the Heart-and-Mind
Of Contending.

JM: This Chapter is strongly reminiscent of *The Art of War*:

> Ultimate Excellence lies not in winning every battle, but in defeating the enemy without ever fighting.

Chang Chung-yuan: One must identify with one's opponent and absorb his strength. When this strength is won, one is bound to Prevail, because the enemy's strength is added to one's own. The Chinese art of Taijiquan and the Japanese art of Aikido both apply this principle. To unify the strength of Others with the strength of Self is also to identify with the Ultimate, which is beyond Space and Time.

Li Bo goes in search of a Hermit in the mountains, and finds him gone and his hermitage deserted.

> *By a stony path*
> *I enter Cinnabar Valley.*
> *The pine gate is choked*
> *With green moss.*
> *There are bird marks*
> *On the deserted steps,*
> *But no one to open the door*
> *Of the Hermit's cell.*
> *I peer through the window*
> *And see his white fly whisk*
> *Hanging on the wall,*
> *Gathering dust.*
> *Disappointed,*
> *I heave a fruitless sigh;*
> *I would leave,*

But loiter wistfully.
Sweet-scented clouds
Drift along the ranges,
Flowers rain from the sky.
Here I taste the bliss of solitude
And listen to the plaint
Of blue monkeys.
Ah, what Calm reigns here,
Remote from all things of the world!

GUEST, NOT HOST

There is a Treatise on War
Which says:
I would rather be Guest
Than Host,
Rather Retreat a foot
Than Advance an inch,
Rather March
The No-March,
Brandish a hand
Without baring an arm,
Thrust
With no Weapon,
Attack
Where there is no Enemy.
The Greatest Disaster
Is to underestimate
The Enemy.

In so doing

I risk losing

My Treasure.

When two armies

Engage in Combat,

The one that feels

Sorrow

Prevails.

THE RIVER MASTER

This is Lao-tzu on War. Lao-tzu disliked the Treatises of his time, such as *The Art of War*.

The Host is the one

Who takes the initiative,

The Aggressor.

The Guest

Responds in Harmony,

Rather than take the lead.

The Taoist

Prefers to be Guest.

The Taoist Warrior follows Heaven-and-Nature and waits before making a move. To Advance an inch is to encroach on enemy territory. The Taoist exploits enemy resources, closes the gates, holds the city, and Retreats a foot. This is to March the No-March.

MAGISTER LIU

The Guest has no Heart-and-Mind of Contending.

The Guest Retreats,

Rather than

Advance,
Causes no Harm
To either side,
Maintains
The Treasure of Compassion
Even in the Fray of War.

This Chapter expands on the notion of Not-Contending, how it Prevails, how the Guest gains the Victory. In the saying quoted by Lao-tzu, the Host is the Aggressor, the one who initiates operations against the Enemy. The Guest waits to respond. To Advance is to seek battle, to Retreat is to avoid battle, to march the No-March. Victory goes to those who Cleave to the Heart-and-Mind of Compassion, who know Sorrow, who do not regard the Harm sustained by Others lightly. This is the Victory of Not-Contending.

Duyvendak: The Host is the one who launches the offensive, while the Guest waits cautiously in Taoist anticipation.

JM: Sun-tzu's *The Art of War* often appropriates the Taoist message, perverting it to support a fundamentally Machiavellian philosophy.

Know the enemy, know yourself, and victory is never in doubt,
not in a hundred battles.

Li Bo sets out from the famous Butterfly Dream of the Taoist Master Zhuang, to Contemplate the Infinite Transformations of the Universe.

Master Zhuang in a dream
Became
A butterfly.
The butterfly
Became
Master Zhuang.
Which was Real—
Butterfly

Or man?
Such is the endless
Transformation of things.
The water
In the distant depths
Of the ocean
Returns to the shallows
Of a limpid stream.
The man growing melons
By Green Gate
Was once
Prince of East Hill.
Rank and riches
Come and go.
And yet we toil and toil—
To what end?

JADE AND SACKCLOTH

My Words are
So easy to
Understand,
They are
So easy to
Practice.
And yet
In All-under-Heaven
No one
Understands them,
No one
Practices them.
My Words have
An Ancestor,
My Deeds have
A Lord.

But no one
Understands them.
Few Understand me at all.
Rare are those
Who pattern themselves
On me.
The Taoist is clad
In brown sackcloth,
But has Jade
In his bosom.

THE RIVER MASTER

The Multitude are averse to the words of Lao-tzu, to the Soft and Gentle, they prefer the Hard and Strong. The Taoist emanates a dark hint of Inner Power, scarcely visible from the outside, infinitely fine and subtle. It is seldom Understood. The few who do Understand Me are One with the Great Tao. Conceal your Treasure in your bosom, do not reveal it to Others.

MAGISTER LIU

The Ancestor and the Lord are the True Tao, the Words and Deeds of the Ancestor and the Lord Flow with the So-of-Itself, with the Way of Nature. Taoists hold their Jade hidden beneath a garment of sackcloth. They Cleave to One Ancestor, One Lord. The three previous Chapters have spoken of Warfare, of the Inner Power of Not-Contending, of the need to soften the harshness of the Heart-and-Mind that Craves Force and Supremacy, of the need to live in the Tao of Non-Action, of Nature, of the So-of-Itself. Few in All-under-Heaven Understand or Practice this Teaching. They value the False and not the True, they are drawn to the Strange and Cunning, not to the Simple Truth. They are estranged from the Tao. The Ancestor and the Lord are the Primal Mother, they are to be found in both Outer Radiance and Inner Marvel. And yet benighted mortals in All-under-Heaven cling to Words, not to Meaning. They see only the Surface of Deeds. How can they Practice the Tao? How can they Understand Me?

> I am the Tao.
> The Tao is Me,
> One with
> The Ancestor and the Lord,
> One with the Outer Radiance,
> With the Inner Marvel,
> With the Tao,
> Jade in the bosom
> Beneath sackcloth.

Waley: Rich people in times of tumult dressed up as peasants and hid their jade treasures under their clothes. Metaphorically "to wear sackcloth" came to mean "to hide one's light under a bushel . . . to keep one's knowledge to oneself."

Li Bo celebrates the age-old Taoist theme of the evanescence of Life.

> *The Living are*
> *Passing Travelers,*
> *The Dead*
> *Return Home.*
> *After a brief sojourn*
> *Betwixt Heaven and Earth,*
> *In the end, alas,*
> *We are but*
> *Dust of Ages Past.*
> *The rabbit in the moon*
> *Pounds Drugs of Immortality*
> *In vain;*
> *Fu-sang,*
> *The Tree of Long Life,*

Is mere kindling.
Bleached bones
Are mute,
Green pines
Know nothing of spring.
Gazing into the past,
Gazing into the future,
I sigh.
What is there to prize
In this fugitive splendor?

KNOWLEDGE AND ILLNESS

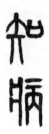

To Know
Not-Knowing,
To Know
That one does not Know,
To Know
That there is a Limit
To what one Knows,
This is
True and Highest
Knowledge.
To deny True Knowledge,
To deny Truth,
Is an Illness.
If this is seen for what it is,
And treated
As an Illness,
It can be cured.
The Taoist
Sees Illness as Illness,
And is healthy.

THE RIVER MASTER

True Knowledge of the Tao
(The Unknowable)
Is the Knowledge
That one does not Know.
This is the Highest Inner Power.

Denial of this True Knowledge may profess to be a kind of Knowledge, but is really a Disease of Inner Power, an Illness. Those who suffer from this Illness, those who profess False Knowledge, can still be healed, they can become healthy again, if they can see it as an Illness. The Taoist sees it for what it is, an Illness, and is healthy in Heart-and-Mind.

The Taoist shares
In the suffering
Of the ignorant.
It is the Taoist's Aspiration
That All-under-Heaven
Should be
Real and Simple,
Should be
Sincere and True,
Should Return
To Pure Nature.

MAGISTER LIU

Highest Knowledge consists in Knowing that there is a Limit to Knowledge. It is an Illness of Heart-and-Mind to be Ignorant and yet to claim Knowledge. Few have the Highest Knowledge. Many suffer from this Illness of Ignorance. Whosoever is able to see it as an Illness can still be healed. The Taoist has this Power, this True Knowledge of the Tao. Highest Knowledge is to Attain Meaning and to forget Words, is to Know No-Knowledge, to seem to Know Nothing. False Knowledge is diseased Knowledge, based on guesswork and cleverness. The Tao cannot be seen or heard, it must be sought within, through Understanding of Underlying Principle, through ever-deepening Self-Cultivation.

The Tao must be Understood
In the Heart-and-Mind,
Through the Light of Spirit,
It will never be found
In columns of Words,
In lists of Precedents,
In Apothegms
Learned by rote,
Without having witnessed
Outer Radiance
And Inner Marvel,
Without Acquaintance
Of the Primal Mother,
With nothing but
Boastful claims
Of Enlightenment
And Perspicacity,
With nothing but
Self-Satisfaction,
With neither Depth
Nor Understanding,
Only Self-Delusion.

Countless scholars of past and present have suffered from this Illness. Those who wish to be Healed must first recognize it for what it is, must distinguish between True and False Knowledge. This is the beginning of Healing. Once they are Healed, then they can grow from Ignorance to True Knowledge, they can be forever free from Disease, they can be healthy and whole.

〻〻

Waley: In the previous Chapter the author calls his own style easy but obscure (no one Understands him), and yet to the Seeker of the Tao who Possesses the Clue his words are perfectly lucid (they are easy to Understand). Here in this Chapter we have the classic example of the "enigmatic lucidity" of Lao-tzu.

JM: Ames and Hall call this "epistemic sclerosis." Li Ling describes the whole Chapter as a "tongue twister" (*raokouling*). Surely he is right. The great Classic, faced yet again with the inadequacy of ordinary logic and language to express the Ineffable Tao, deliberately indulges in word play and near nonsense!

Wang Ji declines a Summons to Office.

> *At the market gate,*
> *I came upon a seller of herbs.*
> *In the mountain garden,*
> *I met a man carrying firewood.*
> *When I can live peacefully*
> *In their company,*
> *Why should I step*
> *Into the Dust and Bustle*
> *Of the world?*

CHERISHING SELF

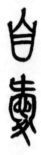

When the folk do not hold
Might in Awe,
Then a Greater Awe
Descends upon them.
Let their dwellings
Not be cramped,
Let their days
Not be made wearisome
By Others,
And they will not
Weary themselves.
The True Taoist
Knows Self,
But does not
Exhibit Self,
Cherishes Self,
But does not
Exalt Self.
Rejects Show,
Knows Self.

THE RIVER MASTER

If men do not fear, if they are not in awe of, the ordinary run-of-the-mill man-ifestations of Might, if they are not cautious and circumspect, then a Great Awe and a Great Harm will descend upon them, the Great Harm of Death and Destruction. A dwelling that is not cramped is a spacious and gentle dwelling of the Heart-and-Mind. Here Spirit can abide. Life-giving Spirit abides in Emp-tiness, takes joy in Clarity and Calm. Whosoever fails to Practice Thrift in daily life, in the consumption of daily food and drink, whosoever injures the Root, and thinks only of Sensual Beauty and Appetite, despising the Tao, will cer-tainly weary and dissipate Spirit. The Taoist is too wise to exhibit the Beauty of Inner Power, and conceals it within. The Taoist Cherishes Self, safeguards Es-sence and Energy, does not Crave Fame and Glory in the World. The Taoist Cleaves to Inner Knowledge, Cherishes True Self.

MAGISTER LIU

To Know Self
Is to have Faith
In Self
Not Others.
To Cherish Self
Is to have
No regrets
About Self,
Not to be
Proud toward Others,
Not to
Exalt Self.

In All-under-Heaven, whosoever does not Understand Self-Cultivation, who-soever Pursues Worldly Power in order to acquire Might, and seeks to be feared and obeyed by Others, is suffering from a grave and stubborn Illness, one that is hard to cure. The only cure is to recognize it for what it is and treat it as an Illness. This is Achieved through Inner Power.

> The Light of Inner Power
> Radiates and Heals.
> Whosoever witnesses
> This Healing
> Is drawn to it,
> Whosoever hears it
> Looks to it
> In admiration.

To Attain this Great Power, be Generous, weigh things with the Generous Measure of Heaven and Earth, be All-Embracing, All-Inclusive, with none of the petty ill feeling that wearies the folk. Feel their Heart-and-Mind as your own, love all things equally, be like the Mother of the Myriad Things, the Ancestor.

> Provide Generous Dwellings
> For all,
> Create Happiness
> For all.
> All of this comes
> From Resonance
> And Inner Power,
> Not from Might.
> There is no Might
> Greater than this.

Wang: When those in authority are unable to control the folk according to the Tao, but instead exercise undue Force, and when the folk can no longer endure their authority [are not in Awe of their Might], then the bond between Ruler and subjects disintegrates, and the terrible judgment of Heaven [a Greater Awe] descends.

Wang Ji sought escape, imbibing True Knowledge of the Tao from the "thing in the cup."

How long
Can this Floating Life
Endure?
How futile
The quest for Hollow Fame!
Better by far
A new vintage,
Another goblet drained
In the Bamboo Grove.

HEAVEN'S NET

The Courage
To Dare
Brings Death;
The Courage
Not to Dare
Preserves Life.
The one Benefits,
The other Harms.
Who can fathom
The Antipathies
Of Heaven-and-Nature?
Even the Taoist
Finds them
Hard to Understand.
The Tao
Of Heaven-and-Nature
Does not Contend,
And yet Prevails,
Says nothing,
And yet is Resonant.
It does not summon,
But things come

Of their own accord;
It is slow,
But lays Plans.
Heaven's Net is vast,
Through its loose Mesh,
Nothing slips.

THE RIVER MASTER

The Courage to Dare is Reckless Action. The Courage Not to Dare is the Caution that Preserves Life. The Inner Power of the True Taoist is averse to Reckless Courage, to Contending, to Words.

Heaven-and-Nature says nothing,
And yet the Myriad Things
Revolve Of-Themselves,
In accord with the Seasons.

The Tao of Heaven-and-Nature is vast and loose, slow and easy, and yet nothing slips through its Net.

MAGISTER LIU

Heaven's Vast Net
Is the Tao.
Heaven-and-Nature
Is silent,
It does not Meddle.
Its Net
Is Non-Action.

Some engage in willful Action. They are bold and daring, recklessly treading on Perilous Terrain and meeting with Death. Others are cautious and prudent, they know when and how to avoid Peril, theirs is a Cautious Courage, they are spared Calamity. They Attain Long Life.

> The Antipathies
> Of Heaven-and-Nature
> Are to be sought out
> In dark and lonely places,
> Places unseen.
> No one Knows why
> The Springs of Change,
> The malign or benign
> Forces of Yin and Yang,
> Of Death and Life,
> Reside
> In these places.

Even the Taoist has difficulty fathoming this. The Taoist Observes the Outer Radiance, Contemplates the Inner Marvel, pays heed to what cannot be seen, to what cannot be heard, extinguishes Desire in Heart-and-Mind. The difference between Daring and Not-Daring, between being Reckless and being Cautious, can hinge on a single thought. Reckless Courage arises in the Heart-and-Mind of Contending, it lies hidden in those dark and lonely places, where Bad Thoughts fester and Good Thoughts are few. We may not be aware of these, but Heaven-and-Nature Knows. We may deceive ourselves, but we can never deceive Heaven-and-Nature.

> The Vast Net
> Of Heaven-and-Nature,
> So vast,
> So wide,
> So loose,
> Gives all their due.
> Not one
> Slips through the Net.

Mathieu: The Plans laid by Heaven are Destiny. Compare this Chapter to "The Heavenly Questions" in the early poetic anthology *Songs of the South*.

JM: In many ways *The Tao and the Power*, which is traditionally thought to have originated in the southern state of Chu, contains echoes of *The Songs of the South*. See for example *Songs*, lines 5–7:

> What manner of things are the darkness and light? How did Yin and Yang come together, and how could they originate and transform all things that are by their commingling?

Duyvendak: The True Courage of the Taoist lies in Not-Daring. Nothing escapes what we would call the Laws of Nature.

Ruan Ji (of the Bamboo Grove) writes to Fu Yi, who has encouraged him to take an official position, of his Taoist Aspirations to transcend the Mundane World, to gather the strings of the Dark Net.

> When a man sets up his aims in life, and finds that the Secret Springs of Destiny do not conform, then he must allow his Spirit to soar, he must raise high his Aspirations and leave the world behind. Letting his Spirit Energy mount on the outer rim of the Realm of Mystery, he elevates his wondrous ambitions beyond the limits of Heaven and Earth, swooping up and down on rays of Light, mounting freely into the heights, in the Transformation of the Tao, moving with the Sun and the Moon. He dwells in No-Room and leaves through No-Gate. At the Great Pole he gathers the strings of the Dark Net, he caresses the Star "Celestial One" in the Inchoate Wastes of Space. The swirling Grime of our world cannot follow in his wake, nor can its flying Dust sully his Purity.

FEAR OF DEATH

When the folk
Do not fear Death,
Why scare them
With Death?
Who would apprehend
The unusual
And put them to Death,
To make Others
Fear Death?
There is already
A Chief Executioner
Charged with
Administering Death.
To take the place
Of the Executioner
Is like chopping
For a Master-Carpenter:
Of those who chop
For the Carpenter
Few escape
Hurting their hands.

THE RIVER MASTER

When the Ruler deals out punishments in a harsh manner, the Well-Being of the folk is affected and they may be driven to such depths of despair that they no longer fear Death. If the Ruler is neither Generous nor Lenient with regard to punishments, and his subjects are slaves to Desire and Greed, what avails it to frighten them with the threat of Death? Lao-tzu is here bemoaning the fact that the Rulers of his time did not seek to Transform their subjects with the Tao and the Inner Power, but instead proceeded at once to harsh punishments.

The Chief Executioner
Administering Death
Is Heaven-and-Nature,
Looking down from above,
Surveying the crimes of mortals.
Nothing slips through its Net.

MAGISTER LIU

Heaven-and-Nature is the Chief Executioner, apportioning Life and Death.

This is the unchanging Way
Of the Tao,
The great Cycle
Of Life and Death.
If a Ruler causes the folk
To Fear Death,
If he utters
The single word *Death*
And takes Life,
This is to abrogate
Heaven's role,
To set foot
On the road to Death.

Whosoever does this is a novice chopping wood for a Master-Carpenter, and risks hurting his hands. Heaven-and-Nature hearkens attentively to every deed in the mortal world, for Good and Evil. Nothing slips through its Net.

So why Meddle, why exert Force on Others? If Heaven-and-Nature cannot force men to be Good, how can men hope to do so? It is a Delusion to think that the folk can be cowed by Fear of Death into doing only what is Good.

> To force them
> To Fear Death,
> Is using Death
> To enhance Death.

It is to make a world in which there is no Life, only Death.

Waley: The Chief Executioner is Heaven, or its agents: pestilence, famine, lightning, earthquake, etc.

Duyvendak: Life and Death are predestined. There is a Chief Executioner in charge—the Tao. If through the Ruler's intervention, Death is inflicted before the predestined moment of Death, the natural course of things is disturbed. This is as dangerous as trying to use the axe of the Master-Carpenter without having learnt his art.

Mathieu: Lao-tzu is criticizing the authoritarian methods of the "proto-legalists," whose ideas finally found expression in the totalitarian reign of the First Emperor of Qin (259–210 BC). These Legalist thinkers misappropriated Taoist ideas for their own ends.

Zhang Fangsheng (fl. AD 386) writes of his Taoist Aspirations toward the Dark Root.

> *I eat the vegetables*
> *In my garden,*
> *I drink my spring wine.*
> *I open my lattice window*
> *And sit gazing*
> *At the river and hills.*
> *Who knows*

My Heart-and-Mind?
I can unburden myself
To no one.
The Unpainted Beam
Is easy to Embrace,
The Dark Root
Never Decays.
Approach it
And it is never far away,
It Endures for ever.

LIFE

The folk
Starve,
While their heavy taxes
Are squandered on food
By those above them.
They are
Hard to Rule,
When those above them
Meddle.
They make light
Of Death,
They trivialize
Death,
When those above them
Pursue Life
Too strenuously.
Those who do not

Pursue Life,
Who abide in
Non-Action,
Are superior to
Those who Cling to Life.

THE RIVER MASTER

The folk starve and freeze because their Ruler has imposed excessive taxes on them. They grow greedy and rebel against the Tao, against the Inner Power. Their Ruler has so many Desires, he Meddles all the time, and so they become like him themselves—

Meddlesome,
Hypocritical,
Hard to Rule.

They trivialize Death. They are bent on Gain and recklessly put their lives in Peril. They endanger themselves, they treat Death lightly and so they enter the Terrain of Death.

MAGISTER LIU

Those who are not engaged in the feverish Pursuit of Life do not trivialize Death, but view it with Calm.

They understand
The Cycle
Of Life and Death
In the light
Of the So-of-Itself,
Of the Tao
Of Heaven-and-Nature.

A Person starves inwardly when the Lord of the Human Heart-and-Mind is obsessed with cravings and schemings, when the False damages the True.

Then Essence and Breath-Energy waste away. But when the Heart-and-Mind of the Tao holds sway, then Life and Death are seen for what they are, the Cycle of Nature, the So-of-Itself.

Chen: This Chapter is a further warning against tyrannical government. When conditions reach an extreme of exploitation and oppression, the folk will naturally rise up in revolt, without any regard to the consequences [they make light of Death].

Chan: This is easily the strongest protest against oppressive government in Chinese literature. It is so strong that it led Hu Shi (1891–1962) to describe Lao-tzu as a rebel.

Ruan Ji meditates on Old Age and the approach of Death:

> *With a sigh*
> *We travel toward Old Age,*
> *In constant sorrow and pain.*
> *At the water's edge*
> *We gaze*
> *At the surging waves,*
> *The many streams that*
> *Flow from One Source.*
> *The hundred years of Life*
> *Would not seem much*
> *Were it not for*
> *Bitterness and hatred,*
> *The Emotions*
> *That trample us down . . .*
> *I will summon*
> *The Darkly Connected One,*
> *Return*
> *To the Tao,*
> *Roam freely*
> *For ever.*

SOFT AND GENTLE

Man,
Born
Soft and Gentle,
Dies
Hard and Rigid.
Of the Myriad Things,
Plants are Born
Soft and Tender,
Die
Dry and Brittle.
The Hard and Rigid are
Companions of Death,
The Soft and Gentle
Companions of Life.
The Forceful Warrior
Meets with Defeat.
Strong Timber
Is cut for Weapons.
Strong and Great
Are Below,

Soft and Gentle
Above.

THE RIVER MASTER

When men are Born, they are Soft and Gently alive with Numinous Breath-
Energy, they Embrace Spirit within. In Death the Breath of Harmony is extinguished, Spirit is lost, they become Hard and Rigid.

All living things,
All herbs and trees,
Are born
Soft and Tender.
The Gentle Breath of Harmony
Abides within them.
When they Die,
That Breath departs,
Leaving them
Dry and Brittle.
The Tao
Of Heaven-and-Nature
Reduces the Strong,
Succors the Gentle.

MAGISTER LIU

Soft and Gentle
Is the Gate of Life,
Hard and Rigid
The Root of Death.
When plants
Push through the soil,
Their shoots are

Soft and Tender,
Burgeoning with Life.
As branches age,
They wither,
The Sap Fails,
And Death
Draws near.

The Forceful and Rigid watch their Essence and Breath-Energy diminish, they watch their Spirit grow dim, they are Companions of Death. The Soft and Gentle reduce Idle Thought and Desire, they do no Harm to Mother Energy, they are Companions of Life.

The I Ching, **Hexagram X, Judgment:**

Stepping on a Tiger's Tail.
Not bitten.
Fortune.
The Soft and Gentle
Step gingerly,
They Endure,
They Prevail
Over the Hard and Strong.

Chan: Weakness, softness, is not only superior to strength. It is the very principle of Life.

Ames and Hall: What is living is soft and supple, and thus flexible; what is dead is hard and rigid, and thus easily broken. It is the weak that is really strong, and it is the strong that is really weak.

Wang Ji drifts like a boat on the Current of Nature.

As evening fades,
I steer my little boat.

The white clouds
Vanish,
The Yellow River
Winds its way back.
Going with the breeze,
I hug the north bank,
Drifting with the waves
Toward the southern isle.
The heaving waters
Surge,
My heart goes wandering afar.
Life is but
A sojourning,
And this
A floating world.
Where are
The Isles of the Immortals?
I sit quietly
Through the autumn of my years.

THE BENT BOW

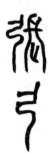

The Tao
Of Heaven-and-Nature
Resembles
A Bent Bow,
Its top
Pushed down,
Its bottom
Raised up,
Excess
Reduced,
Insufficiency
Made good.
The Tao
Of Heaven-and-Nature
Reduces Excess,
Makes good
Insufficiency.
Lesser mortals,
To the contrary,
Decrease Insufficiency,
Increase Excess.

Only the Taoist
Gives that which he possesses
In Excess
To All-under-Heaven.
The Taoist Accomplishes
But does not
Hold on to Action,
Does not abide in
Accomplishment,
Does not wish to
Display his Worth.

THE RIVER MASTER

Dark is the Tao
Of Heaven-and-Nature.
A Bent Bow
Well adjusted,
Well balanced,
Generous Harmony
And Moderation.

Lesser Mortals take from the poor to give to the rich. The Taoist Ruler forgoes Honor and Wealth, and gives Generously to All-under-Heaven without expecting any recompense. He shares Inner Power, Accomplishing but not abiding in Accomplishment, never seeking the admiration of Others.

MAGISTER LIU

This is the Tao
Of the Bent Bow,

The Tao
Of Heaven-and-Nature,
The Return
To the Primal Root,
To the Inchoate Mist,
To the Mystery of Light.
Poised and flexible,
In Perfect Balance,
Every Excess reduced,
Every Insufficiency made good.

Lesser Humans take from Insufficiency, and add to Excess. Cares and Idle Thoughts arise, Essence is dissipated and Spirit wasted. The False prospers. The Taoist loves everything without exception, from the very Root of Heart-and-Mind, expecting no recompense.

Wilhelm: The Chinese Bow bends inwards when it is unstrung, and has to be pressed outwards when strung. [He adds a couple of diagrams, and refers the reader to Chapter 22, about the Curved and the Twisted.]

Waley (disagreeing with Wilhelm): "The Bow is Bent not in the act of stringing, but in the act of shooting an arrow."

Edmund Ryden: The image of firing an arrow from a Longbow is used to illustrate how the Tao of Heaven works to bring Balance to the World. The archer pulls the string and the Bow bends at top and bottom. The string is stretched and then released to power the arrow. The Tao and the Taoist work in the same fashion, constantly adjusting to the nature of the material, and not overstretching anything.

Wang Ji reflects on the need to Retreat, using words from the Ninth Chapter of Lao-tzu.

Stop pouring
At the right time
Into an upright vessel.

That's better by far
Than filling it
To the brim.
Don't hammer
An iron bar
Too hard,
Or the edge won't last.
If you stuff
A hall
With jade and gold,
The treasure can't be kept
Intact.
The Pride of Wealth and Rank
Brings naught but
Calamity.
Achieve, and then
Retreat—
Such is the Tao
Of Heaven.

THE GENTLE PREVAILS

In All-under-Heaven
Nothing is
Softer and Gentler
Than Water.
And yet it Prevails over
The Hard and Strong,
It is invincible.
Nothing Prevails
With such Ease,
Gentle over Strong,
Soft over Hard.
All-under-Heaven
Knows this Truth,
And yet no one
Practices it.
So the Taoist says:

"Whosoever is willing to
Accept the Nation's Filth
Will be Lord
Of the Earth-Altar;
Whosoever is willing to
Absorb the Nation's Misfortune
Will be King
Of All-under-Heaven."
Truths like these
Sound paradoxical.

THE RIVER MASTER

Contained within a circle, Water is round. Within a Square, it is square. When dammed, it is Still. When unleashed, it Moves. Water, softest of all things, wraps itself round mountains, it causes hills to move. It wears through iron and dissolves copper.

Nothing Prevails
Over Water.
Water
Extinguishes fire.
Yin dissolves Yang.
The tongue is Soft,
The teeth are Hard,
The teeth Perish
Before the tongue.
Soft and Gentle Endure.

All-under-Heaven knows this to be True, but is too ashamed of being humble, is too attached to Pride and Power, and so refuses to Practice it.

MAGISTER LIU

Soft and Gentle
Prevail.
Water wends its way
Gently
Round every obstacle,
Avoids Heights,
Sinks to Depths,
Bends with curves,
Fills and pours,
Fits into Square and Circle,
Into Small and Great,
Into springs and rivers,
Smoothing the Surface of things,
Accepting all manner of Filth,
Containing gold,
Extinguishing fire,
Bringing Life
To plants and trees,
Softening and moistening
The soil,
Bringing Benefit
To the Myriad Things,
Never Contending,
Always lower,
Always beneath
All-under-Heaven,
Supremely
Soft and Gentle.
Solid Earth
Collapses
When infiltrated by Water.
Weighty Mountains
Crumble
Under a flood of Water.
Fierce Fire

Is extinguished
By Water.
Nothing Prevails
Against Water.

The Taoist is Soft and Gentle as Water, lying Beneath not Above, absorbing Filth, accepting Misfortune and Calamity. Unexpected Hardships overwhelm Others, but are overcome by the Soft and Gentle Taoist. This is the paradox, the Truth: that Soft and Gentle Prevail over Hard and Strong. The Multitude admire the Hard and Strong. But whosoever sees by the Light of the Primal Mother Understands this Truth, Knows that Water, Softest of all things, is the Exemplar of the Tao.

Waley: The Nation's Filth is the clod of earth taken from the Royal Altar of Soil and Grain, which was presented to a feudal lord as a token of his investiture, so as to erect with it an Altar of Soil and Grain in his own fief. A Ruler who absorbs the Misfortune of a Nation inherits the evil omens of a conquered state, and turns them to his own advantage.

Wang Ji muses on a Taoist theme before dawn one spring morning.

The spring night
Has long to go.
Through my high window
Shines
The bright moon.
Sleepless
I toss and turn,
I throw on my gown,
Pace about at the front door,
My Heart,
For the moment,
Is undisturbed,
My Body and Mind
Are Pure.

I muse
On the distant past,
I survey
The affairs of today.
Pure and foul—
In the end
How do they differ?
All is but
A Cycle of Fate.
Through my myriad sighs
I hear the morning rooster crow.
To abandon Artifice
Is to preserve
Essence,
Is to be moored
In Calm.

HOLDING THE TALLY

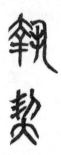

Harmonize
Great Bitterness,
And some Bitterness
Will yet remain.
How can this be
Mended?
The Taoist
Holds the left-hand Tally
But never calls Others
To account.
Whosoever has
Inner Power
Is Content
To hold the Tally.
Whosoever lacks
Inner Power
Calls in debts.
The Tao
Of Heaven-and-Nature
Makes no distinctions,

Is always Generous
To the Good.

THE RIVER MASTER

If we rely on punishment to Harmonize and mollify, some Resentment and Bitterness will always remain. The Taoists of Old were Generous, they simply kept the left-hand Tally to assure a Contract.

> They had
> No documents,
> No laws.
> The notched Tally
> Was their only
> Surety.

In this way the one with Inner Power ensures that all is fair, while the one without Inner Power ruthlessly inflicts Loss on Others. The Tao of Heaven-and-Nature is Generous, it honors contracts in a Soft and Gentle way.

MAGISTER LIU

In any Contract, the creditor keeps the left-hand Tally, and the debtor keeps the right-hand Tally. Inner Power is its own Tally, a surety in which Non-Action, the So-of-Itself, Prevails. Whosoever lacks Inner Power will try to control Others by Force, will demand a due, exact a tithe, and Bitterness will ensue. The Tao of Softness and Gentleness wards off Bitterness. Hardness and Strength, Vanity and Pride, create Bitterness and Resentment. Hardness remains buried deep within. Its Root cannot be removed.

> As in a Mirror,
> Taoists Observe
> The Outer Radiance,

Contemplate
The Inner Marvel,
Transforming Energy and Spirit
With Calm,
Never doing to Others
What they would not wish
To have done to themselves.
They hold
The left-hand Tally
But do not call in a debt.
They
Let it Go,
They do not think of it
As a Tithe
To be collected.

Waley: The Taoist is like the holder of the left hand of a tally, ready to give out what is due (i.e., ready to vouchsafe the bounties of the Tao), but not making claims on others, like a creditor. He is like the officer who gives public assistance to the needy and aged, whereas the ordinary Ruler is a sort of Grand Tithe-Collector. The Taoist has been supplied with the inexhaustible treasures of the Tao, and can therefore be Generous.

Xi Kang, blacksmith-musician of the Bamboo Grove, in his "Rhapsody on the Lute," recognizes the Inner Power of Music to Harmonize Emotion and foster Inner Calm.

Since my youth I have loved Music,
Have practiced it all my life.
Things Prosper and Decay,
But Music never changes,
Music Endures.
Tastes may satiate,
But Music never palls.
It Guides and Nurtures

Spirit,
It Elevates and Harmonizes
Emotion,
It brings Solace
To the wretched . . .
Music surpasses
All the Arts.

TYING KNOTS

In a Small Nation
With few folk,
Tools abound,
But are not put to use.
The folk,
Mindful of Death,
Never journey far.
Boats and carriages
Are not used for travel.
Weapons and soldiers
Are not deployed.
The folk Return
To the Ancient Tying of Knots.
They think their simple diet
Sweet,
Their raiment
Fine.
They find Peace
In their dwellings,
Joy

In their customs.

Neighboring countries

Can be seen,

Cocks are heard crowing,

Dogs barking.

The folk

Die of Old Age

Happy where they are,

Without ever having

Traveled.

THE RIVER MASTER

The Taoist Ruler thinks of a Large Nation as Small, and is Thrifty concerning details. The Taoist Ruler does not Meddle, and the folk are Content with Life, they feel no need to leave their homes.

Their boats and carriages

Are not needed.

There is Clarity and Calm,

Non-Action,

No outward show,

The folk do not covet

The pleasures of Others.

Weapons are not deployed.

In All-under-Heaven

There is no Hatred,

No Resentment.

The folk return to Simple Tying of Knots for daily use, to Simple Reality, they are Sincere and free from Falsity.

They find Peace

In their reed-huts.

They do not crave
Ornamented dwellings.
They find Joy
In their Simple Customs,
And have no Desire
To change them.

They reach Old Age and Death without ever having mingled with the people of their neighboring Nation. They have no Desire to do so.

MAGISTER LIU

From the Great,
The Tao Returns
To the Small.
From the Many
To the Few.
The Tao is Woman,
Not Man.
It Returns
To the Purity
Of the Uncarved Block.
Abiding in Non-Action,
The folk are
Content.
They are
In the Dust
But not
Of the Dust,
They are
In the World
But not
Of the World.

They neither see nor hear the beautiful sounds and sensual sights before them. They are not of the Dust, they are not contained or defined by it.

In the end the Multitude Return to the True Strength of the Soft and Gentle, the Soft within the Hard, the Hard within the Soft, the Gentle within the Strong, the Strong within the Gentle.

> This is a Return
> To a Balanced World,
> To the Primal Root,
> To Life-Destiny.
> This is the Tao
> Of Fulfilled Inner Nature,
> Of Contentment.

The Embryo of the Tao is formed, through the Soft and Gentle Practice of Contemplation, of Self-Cultivation. A Small Nation is a Soft and Gentle Realm, one in which the folk do not travel far. Their Heart-and-Mind is all Clarity and Calm. They Cleave to the Tao, to Non-Action. They are Busy about No-Business. They are Content. Boats belong to Action, Weapons are Instruments of Meddling. Such things are not needed in the Realm of Non-Action and No-Meddling. Putting all such things aside, the folk find Peace in Nature, in the So-of-Itself, in True Resonance and Calm, just as in Ancient Times men kept records with Knotted Ropes, and suffered no hindrance as a consequence.

> The folk die Content
> In Old Age,
> Hearing the Sound
> Of No-Sound,
> Seeing the Sight
> Of No-Sight.
> This is the Solitary Grain
> In the Vast Void,
> Round and Bright,
> Calm and Naked.
> All is
> In the Heart-and-Mind.

Duyvendak: This Chapter gives a description of the ideal state without culture. For the criticism of labor-saving devices compare *The Book of Taoist Master Zhuang*, Chapter 12, where the use of a clever device for drawing water from a well, a wooden well-sweep, is condemned by an old gardener.

> I've heard my Teacher say, where there are machines, there are bound to be machine worries. Where there are machine worries there are bound to be machine hearts. With a machine heart, you've spoiled what was Pure and Simple.

Waley: One knots ropes as an aid to one's own memory (compare our "tying a knot in one's handkerchief"), whereas one writes contracts down in order to make other people fulfill them. That, I think, is why "knotting" belongs to the Golden Age.

The monk-poet Jiaoran (730–799) meditates on living in the World with Hidden Heart-and-Mind.

> *I hide*
> *My Heart-and-Mind,*
> *Not my Tracks.*
> *I love to live*
> *In the World of Men.*
> *If there are*
> *Too few trees,*
> *I plant one in springtime,*
> *If there are*
> *No mountains,*
> *I paint one.*
> *I never complain of*
> *Noise.*
> *Truth is here*
> *In its midst.*

THE LEARNED DO NOT UNDERSTAND

Trustworthy words
Are not Beautiful,
Beautiful words
Are not to be Trusted.
The Good
Do not Dispute,
Those who Dispute
Are not Good.
Those who Understand
Are not Learned,
The Learned
Do not Understand.
Taoists
Do not Hoard,
The more they give to Others,

The more they have.
The more they share,
The more is theirs.
The Tao of Heaven
Brings Benefit,
Never Harm.
The Taoist Accomplishes,
But never Contends.

THE RIVER MASTER

Trustworthy words are
Simple and Real.
Beautiful words are
Outwardly seductive,
But False and Hollow.
Those who
Understand the Tao
Are not
Learned,
They Embrace
The One,
The Primordial.

The Learned see and hear a great deal, but they do not Understand. The Good practice Self-Cultivation in the Tao, they have no outward show of elegance.

Those who Dispute
Utter crafty Words,
Creating nothing
But Sorrow
With their tongues.

The Taoist accumulates Inner Power but does not hoard Wealth, uses Inner Power to instruct the foolish, gives Wealth away to the poor and has all the more.

The Bounty
Of the Tao
Is Infinite,
Like the inexhaustible
Splendor
Of Sun and Moon.

MAGISTER LIU

The Taoist Accomplishes but never Contends. The Five Thousand Words of this book can be summed up in the Word "Not-Contending." The Taoist's Aspiration on behalf of future generations in All-under-Heaven is that they will never again Contend. The previous Eighty Chapters of this book Transmit the voice of the Taoists of Old, Perfecti of the Primordial Word, who bore witness to both Outer Radiance and Inner Marvel. The voice of the Primal Mother can be heard in every word. Ponder these words, savor their deeper meaning. This is a Song in Praise of Taoist Compassion, concerning which the Perfecti have already given instruction. The book's Five Thousand Words are beautifully written, but theirs is not a Contrived Beauty. These are Simple Words of the Tao and of the Inner Power. They are Beautiful to the ear, but they are also Trustworthy in their Substance. These Five Thousand Words may seem to Dispute, but their Disputation is not Contrived. They Return to Purity, to the Uncarved Block. In these Five Thousand Words, there is much use of Ancient Sayings. This may appear Learned, but it is not a Contrived Learning. These Ancient Sayings Illuminate the Present. Taoists wish to share their Inner Power with All-under-Heaven, with future generations. The more they share with Others, the more they have for themselves. Humanity and Human Relations are at the core of the Five Thousand Words of this book. The Ancestor of the Tao, the Father of Compassion, is Supremely Good. I can find no proper way to Name him. If obliged to use Words, I can only speak of the Tao of Not-Contending.

Chan: As if this Chapter were meant to be a general conclusion to the book, the basic ideas of Simplicity, the One, the Tao of Heaven-and-Nature, are all reiterated. As Wang Bi has said, the basis of Beauty lies in Simplicity, and the basis of Knowledge, in Unity, in the One.

Master Zhuang: The fish trap exists because of the fish. Once you've caught the fish, forget the trap. The rabbit snare exists because of the rabbit. Once you've caught the rabbit, forget the snare. Words exist because of Meaning. Once you've caught the Meaning, forget the Words.

Ruan Ji meditates on the Futility of Learning, on how the Learned do not Understand.

> *Long years ago,*
> *At fifteen, maybe less,*
> *How earnestly*
> *I loved the Classics then.*
> *Poor as I was, my heart*
> *Possessed True Wealth,*
> *That ache to learn such Truths*
> *As make good men.*
> *I threw all windows*
> *Wide upon the world*
> *And climbed high hills*
> *To find those Truths I sought.*
> *The heights were knobbed*
> *With grave-mounds.*
> *Hundreds and hundreds*
> *Of hundreds and hundreds*
> *All brought down to naught.*
> *Thousands of thousands of thousands*
> *Of years from now*
> *What will a Fair Name count for?*
> *Nothing at all.*
> *At last I understand*
> *Earth's oldest wisdom*
> *And laugh out loud*
> *At that lad*
> *Who was*
> *Learning's thrall.*

A TAOIST FLORILEGIUM

Gleanings of the Tao

Taoist Self-Cultivation:
Adept with Inner Infant

To help readers new to the Taoist way of thinking, and to illustrate certain of the book's key Images and Themes, I have selected a few flowers and woven them together, from both the original text and the Commentaries.

TAO

The word *Tao* was translated by the Jesuit Father Régis as *Vis Operativa et Operandi, Via, Ratio, Lex*. The Tao is "the unnameable in union with which we are spontaneously on course." The Great Tao is complete. With Good Faith and Kindness, one sees the Myriad Things as one great entity; one sees Self and Other as one great Family. It is like the Wind blowing . . . Everything dances before it. Ignorance of the Great Tao is a darkened, deserted house, it is conceit, it is self-satisfaction, vain embellishment of the façade. This gaudy shrine contains no Buddha. It is ultimately Ineffable and thus cannot be "understood" cognitively. Even though the Tao cannot be known intellectually, because it is fundamental to all Being, it can be experienced and embodied.

INNER POWER

This is the Inner Strength or *mana* that flows from the experience of the True Tao. The Greater Knowledge which resembles Folly, the Greater Cleverness which resembles Clumsiness, provide a path to a Higher Heart-and-Mind, to the Inner Power of the Tao. To Cultivate this Power, one must go beyond Attachment and Action, to the Heart-and-Mind of the Tao, which cannot be seen, which cannot be heard, which has no Form, which leaves no Trace. This is the Mystic Power of the Infant. The Power is the Tao, the Tao is the Power. To discard Learning is to Cultivate Inner Power, to be Nourished by the Mother is to follow the Tao. The Power never ceases to be Calm even in Motion, it never ceases to be One with the Tao. Inner Power Radiates and Heals. This Inner Power is the fruit of Self-Cultivation, it is the manifestation of the Tao. It is the personal capacity to carry out the most Harmonious course of Action, or Non-Action. Cultivate Heart-and-Mind, let it be unmoved by sorrow and joy, Know that certain things are inevitable. This is the height Of Spiritual Strength. Inner Strength is the only True Source of Teaching. It makes Connections. It is an uninterrupted current, one and the same Water, passing from one place to another. It reaches everywhere. The True Gentleman practices the Tao, building Inner Power, Inner Strength, taking every step in a measured way. It is like Water flowing easily from one place to another. His every word is well considered. He is at peace, like a Lake on which no wave stirs. When he acts, he never loses touch with his Inner Nature.

SELF-CULTIVATION

Self-Cultivation is Mastery of the Heart-and-Mind. It covers a wide range of Practices. These include paradoxical thinking along the lines of the Taoist Masters, stretching the Heart-and-Mind beyond "normal" confines, psychological practices (various forms of yoga, plain "sitting," and still meditation), sexual or dietetic practices, and basic ethical principles, such as living according to Moderation and in Harmony with Nature. Self-Cultivation in the broadest sense also includes such activities as calligraphy, painting, and literature—in fact all of the arts, when carried out "in the Tao." The Alchemical Work is Achieved through Self-Cultivation. The Embryo of the Tao is formed through the Soft and Gentle Practice of Contemplation. The Taoist stills Desire through the Great Tao, keeps Spirit Whole and safe from Harm. This is to put aside Human Heart-and-Mind, and to Attain the Heart-and-Mind of the Tao. Self-Cultivation Returns first to the Infant, then to the Infinite, finally to the Uncarved Block, the True Elixir itself, in which the Tao is Whole. This is to be One with Emptiness, with Non-Action. Spirit can be Transformed only through Inner Power, not through Action. The Work of Genuine Understanding, the proper Work of Self-Cultivation, requires the peeling away of layer upon layer, until one reaches the Marrow of the Tao, True Knowledge, Clear Perception. Just as Water is drawn from the Well, so too the numinous content deep in the soul is drawn upward into consciousness through Self-Cultivation.

SO-OF-ITSELF

This is the Inner Power of Primal Radiance, the Gateway of All Marvels. It cannot be seen, it cannot be known, it cannot be Named. If we have to give it a Name, we call it the So-of-Itself, we call it Nature. For the True Seekers of the Tao, who Nurture Life, there is no Terrain of Death. Inner Power, Mystic Power, in its Non-Being, in its Non-Action, is invisible, is unknowable, it Nourishes them, brings them to Fulfillment, to Completion. They Return to Nature, to the So-of-Itself. Heaven models itself on the Tao, the Clear, the Calm and Silent. The Tao models itself on Nature, the So-of-Itself. The Tao is Nature. It has no other model.

TRANSFORMATION OF HUMAN HEART-AND-MIND

White Light shines in an Empty Room, the Inner Marvel of Illumination is Born of Outer Radiance. All is in the Heart-and-Mind. It is a solitary grain in the Vast Void, Round and Bright, Calm and Naked. The wiles of the Human Heart-and-Mind are thorns and brambles, futile expense of Spirit, a poor harvest. The Taoist Returns Home, to Nature, to the So-of-Itself, and thereby keeps Heart-and-Mind safe from Harm. This is the Transformation of the Tao. Brambles are Transformed into healing herbs, the poor harvest into an Abundance.

OBSERVATION AND CONTEMPLATION

Magister Liu stresses the importance of the stage of Observation in Self-Cultivation, whereby the Taoist first perceives the working of the Tao in the outer physical world, then proceeds to Inner Contemplation of its Marvels. In freedom from Desire, we look within and Contemplate the Inner Marvel, not with eyes but inwardly by the Light of Spirit. Looking outward, with the eyes of Desire, we Observe the Outer Radiance. Desire itself is born within the Heart-and-Mind, in the first Inklings, in the embryonic Springs of Thought. I am the Tao. The Tao is Me, One with the Ancestor and the Lord, One with the Outer Radiance, with the Inner Marvel, with the Tao, the Jade in the bosom beneath Sackcloth.

BREATH-ENERGY

This is Vitality, Life Breath or Vital Breath. Joseph Needham calls it *pneuma*, or matter-energy. It is a fundamental concept in the whole range of Chinese traditional thinking. It is the basic substance out of which the entire universe is composed. Human beings have some measure of control over the rate at which their original endowment of Breath-Energy (*qi*) stagnates or is depleted. Balance of Breath-Energy in the mental and emotional spheres can be Achieved by Self-Cultivation. Various techniques designed to retain (and ideally augment) Breath-Energy include both moral and physical arts: moderation in daily habits, adjustment of posture, meditation as "inward training" or Self-Cultivation, habituation to goodness, and a calm acceptance of fate. Breath-Energy is a force that expands and animates the world in a turning motion, in the revolutions by which it spreads and distributes itself into every corner of Space and Time.

HEART-AND-MIND

This translation (rather than either "heart" or "mind") reflects the blending of belief and desire (thought and feeling, ideas and emotions) in the Chinese word *xin*. This English word is singular (The Heart-and-Mind *is . . .*) and has nothing whatsoever to do with winning over "Hearts and Minds." The Human Heart-and-Mind must be restrained by the Heart-and-Mind of the Tao. Expel Cleverness, Treasure the Light within. A man's True Yin and Yang become Dispersed when he clings to the Human Heart-and-Mind, and abandons the Heart-and-Mind of the Tao. Every step down this path leads further toward Danger. Embrace the Heart-and-Mind of the Tao, let go of the Human Heart-and-Mind, take hold of the Jewel of Life in the Tiger's Lair, the Bright Pearl in the Dragon's Pool (enlightenment in the mundane world).

NON-ACTION

This is not idly "doing nothing," the lazy attitude of a *fainéant*, but the re-laxed, effortless attitude of the Taoist, who seems to "do" nothing, but actu-ally does a great deal, because he is naturally in Harmony with the Tao. Things just Happen. The folk Return to Calm, to Simplicity and Purity. They find Peace in Non-Action, in the Rhythms of Nature. With True Knowledge, Action is Eschewed, and all is Accomplished through Non-Action, through the Pure Breath-Energy of the Tao. The Taoist Accomplishes through Non-Action, through the So-of-Itself, the Way of Nature. The Taoist is Busy about No-Business, tastes No-Taste with the dispassionate appreciation of the con-noisseur, with Clarity and Calm. The Master is Calm, his is the magical pas-sivity that is also called Non-Action. The Tao is Non-Action. With it the Myriad Things are Transformed and effortlessly become Whole, according to the So-of-Itself. This is the True Benefit of Non-Action, the Soft and Gentle Tao. This Wordless Teaching is learned from Self-Cultivation in Non-Action.

NOT-CONTENDING

Not-Contending is Non-Action. Through Not-Contending, Water Benefits the Myriad Things. Therein lies its Excellence. Every Excellence (in dwelling, in Heart-and-Mind, in friendship, in words) resembles that of Water, which does not Contend. This is the Excellence of the Inner Power of the Tao, which resembles that of Water.

NO-KNOWLEDGE

The Taoist has this Powerful and True Knowledge of the Tao. Highest Knowl-edge is to Attain Meaning and to forget Words, is to Know No-Knowledge, to seem to Know Nothing.

NON-BEING, EMPTINESS

With the Return to the Primal, to the Root, to where Non-Being and Being are once again One, the World's Hurly-Burly grows quiet. Being and Substance bring Benefit; Non-Being and Emptiness make things Useful. This is the opposite of Being; it is the formless, undifferentiated Void or Chaos out of which Being comes. It is in going "back" to that Non-Being, in the Return to that Root, that the Taoist seeks his Life-Destiny.

WATER

This is the Prime Symbol of the Tao. Water is close to the Tao. It resembles the Woman who lies Beneath the Man. Dammed, it comes to a Halt; released, it Flows. It follows and obeys. This is its Nature. None can find fault with Water. Whosoever sees by the Light of the Primal Mother Understands this Truth, Knows that Water is the Exemplar of the Tao. The Heart-and-Mind finds Excellence in Calm and in Freedom from Desire, in Depth, just as Water finds Calm in a still, unruffled pond. Just as Water brings moisture to every place, so too the Taoist sees all as equals, close friends and distant persons alike, brings Peace to the elderly, Cherishes the young. Water wends its way gently round every obstacle, avoids height, sinks to depths, bends with curves, fills and pours, fits into Square and Circle, into Small and Great, into springs and rivers, smooths the Surface of things, accepts all manner of filth, contains gold, extinguishes fire, brings Life to plants and trees, softens and moistens the soil, brings Benefit to the Myriad Things, never Contending, always lower, always beneath All-under-Heaven, Supremely Soft and Gentle.

MOTHER, WOMAN, THE MYSTERIOUS FEMININE

The Son Returns to the Mother, Cleaves to her. The Son knows the Man, but Cleaves to the Woman. The Son is Nourished by the Mother, builds strength from softest shoots, from tiniest details. Woman Prevails through lying Beneath, through Calm, Prevails through Softness, over the Hard, over Man. When Man unites with Woman, Hard submits to Soft, Hard is contained within Soft. The Primal Mother's voice can be heard in every word. The Taoist, like Woman, is Quiet and Still, is Soft and Tender.

FLOOD, OCEAN

The Flood of the Tao is like water blown by the wind, like waves rippling to left and right, coming forth and disappearing in unfathomable ways. I drift and glide, like the boundless floods of River and Ocean, seeking repose in the Realm of Spirit. My Heart-and-Mind Drifts in the Tao, my only Home. Others busily Contend, wasting Spirit. Others sparkle and are bright, I am dull and listless, like the boundless Ocean.

VALLEY SPIRIT

Consider two mountain peaks facing each other, and the Valley between. A voice calls out, an echo replies, a Sound from Nothingness, a Something without Form, neither a Nothing nor a Something, a concentration of Pure Breath-Energy. This is the Valley Spirit.

RAVINE, ABYSS

The Tao is fathomless and unknowable, like Water deep in an Abyss. Be Humble and Lowly, like a Deep Ravine, and the Power will be Constant. All-under-Heaven Comes Home to the One, like Water pouring into a Deep Ravine. Know Man, Cleave to Woman. Be a Ravine for All-under-Heaven, with Constant Power that never fades. Be Humble and Lowly, like a Deep Ravine, and the Power will be Constant.

DUST, IN THE WORLD

Dust is a common metaphor for the noise and fuss of the World, of everyday life. Taoism in its true sense calls for identification with, not an escape from, the World ("merging with the Dust"), all the while keeping the Light of the Tao Dark, not letting it shine. Be One with the Dust of the World, blend with it, do not stay aloof. This is the Mystic Union of Heaven-and-Nature, to be One with the Tao. The Taoist often conceals his Treasure, and lives hidden in the crowd. But once met, he kindles Light in others. Dwell in the world, do not deny it, Merge with the Dust, Resonate with outer things, be still and not entangled, in the Dust but not of the Dust, in the World but not of the World. The True Gentleman, who practices the Tao, gathers his Vital Spirit, vast as the Heavens. He learns to live in the World without injuring Spirit. He dwells in the Dust but is able to rise above the Dust.

BELLOWS

Like Air from a Bellows, Infinite Breath-Energy issues from the Emptiness of the Tao. The Bellows works through the Tao of Non-Action between Heaven and Earth, through the Wordless Tao, through Emptiness. Utter No Words, Hold Fast to the Center. This is the Bellows, the Tao of Heaven and Earth.

BENT BOW

Dark is the Tao of Heaven-and-Nature, it is a Bent Bow well adjusted, Generous Harmony and Moderation. This is the Tao of the Bent Bow, of Heaven-and-Nature, the Return to the Primal Root, to the Inchoate Mist, the Mystery of Light Concealed.

INFANT

Abundant Inner Power resembles an Infant, whom poisonous insects do not sting, whom fierce beasts do not seize, whom birds of prey do not attack. The Infant's bones and sinews are Soft, but its grasp is Sure. The Infant knows nothing of the joining of Woman and Man, and yet its member can stand erect. Its Essence is Perfect. All day the Infant may cry, but is never hoarse. Its Harmony is Perfect. The Heart-and-Mind of the Tao, of the Infant, is One. It has no Two, no Division, no False Knowledge, only the Primordial Power of the Ancients. With the Greater Knowledge which resembles Folly, with the Greater Cleverness which resembles Clumsiness, this Power of the Infant is the path to a Higher Heart-and-Mind, to the Inner Power of the Tao.

FOOL

The Mystic Power of the Taoist is deep and distant, it cannot be sought out by Taught Illumination, it cannot be Attained by so-called Wisdom. It is reached through sheer Folly, Returning with things to their Source, to the Tao, following Gently in the Grand Flow. The Taoists of Old did not seek

Illumination by way of False Knowledge and Cunning, but instead sought the Transformation that comes of Folly. This brought Clarity and Calm to their thinking. The Taoist deals quietly with All-under-Heaven, with the Heart-and-Mind of a Fool.

ROOT, SOURCE, ORIGIN

The Root of the Tao proceeds from Void, from Non-Being, it is the Origin, the Source of Heaven and Earth, Mother of the Myriad Things, Nurturing All-under-Heaven, as a Mother Nurtures her Children. The Myriad Modes of Being share a Single Root, like the many Streams and Valleys which Return Home to the Great River and the Ocean, like the thousands of Threads, the Myriad Strands, which are One Tao, One Uncarved Block.

EMBRACING THE ONE

Wholeness is Achieved by Attaining the One. Without the One, Things Fail. The One is the True Breath-Energy contained within the Supreme Ultimate, it is the Mother of the Myriad Things, it is itself without Form but sets Form in Motion. The One enables everything to be what it is—Heaven, Earth, Spirit, the Valley. Without the One, Kings lose Authority, they Tumble, however high their Rank. The One is Root and Foundation of all.

UNCARVED BLOCK

Symbol of the "primal undifferentiated unity underlying the apparent complexity of the universe." To Return Home to the Uncarved Block, to the Inchoate Fog, to the Infant, is to put aside the Human Heart-and-Mind, and to Attain the Heart-and-Mind of the Tao. The Uncarved Block Transforms Heart-and-Mind. Be Simple, like a Block of Uncarved Wood; be Broad as a

Valley, Murky as Mud. The Taoists were like Mud that settles and becomes clear. They Attained Calm but were lively in Gentle Motion.

SIMPLE UNDYED SILK, KNOTTED CORDS

Like the Uncarved Block, Simple Silk is a symbol of the "attributeless" nature of the Tao, a Return "from the dead letter of moral precepts" to a Taoist state of Simplicity without Culture or Artifice. It resembles the Simplicity of the Three Most August Ones of Ancient Days, who communicated with Knotted Cords and dispensed with writing altogether.

BINDING STRAND

With the Binding Strand of the Tao, among its Countless Transformations, Being Returns to Non-Being in the Free Flow of Nature, Returns to the One with No Substance which dwells in its midst, to the Ancient Beginning that Binds.

HEAVEN'S NET

Heaven's Net is the Tao. Heaven-and-Nature is silent, it does not Meddle. Its Net is Non-Action.

LINEAGE OF THE LIGHT

There is a Higher Knowledge deep within the sense of being lost, a Knowledge that is No-Knowledge. Its Transmission is the Lineage of Light, which stems directly from Nature, from the So-of-Itself. This is a Great Mystery. The Lineage of Light is transmitted from Teacher to Disciple. If the Disciple does not esteem his Teacher, if the Teacher does not care to Teach, then the Transmission is broken and the way is lost, however hugely knowledgeable and clever and wise one may think oneself to be. To Understand this is to Understand a Great Mystery of the Tao.

SMALL FISH, NOT-MEDDLING

So the True Taoist says: I change nothing, and the folk are Transformed and Perfected. I do not Meddle, and they prosper Of-themselves. It is One, not Two, it is Dark, it does not shine. The Large is Hard and Forceful, the Small is Soft and Gentle. To Rule a Large Nation in the manner of cooking a small fish is to use the Soft and Gentle to pacify the Hard and Forceful. Do not handle a small fish too much, in case it disintegrates. If the Rulers of a Nation Meddle, the folk will be distressed.

LIFE-DESTINY

This is the Self-Perfection that Heaven has given a person, to accomplish which is the consummation of all Taoist practice. It can also be translated as Life-Store, the Font of Vitality, the store of Vital Forces of a human being that are wasted in such things as Sex, Violent Emotion, and Desire, all of which cause the vital fluids (sexual fluids, sweat, saliva, moist breath) to drain away. When this Life-Store is exhausted, the result is Death.

MYRIAD THINGS

Everything that exists, all objects or external phenomena.

ALL-UNDER-HEAVEN

Literally, the World "Beneath Heaven," all things and peoples, the entire world known to the Chinese.

HEAVEN-AND-NATURE

Literally Heaven, but in a broader sense Nature, the course which things follow or should follow—the recurrence of the Seasons, the cycles of the Heavenly Bodies, the Tao of Heaven-and-Nature. Everything which man cannot alter—his Nature, his Destiny—is due to the Decree of Heaven.

LIFE AND DEATH

Taoists understand the Cycle of Life and Death in the light of the So-of-Itself, of the Tao of Heaven-and-Nature. When the Heart-and-Mind of the Tao holds sway, then Life and Death are seen for what they are: the Cycle of Nature, the So-of-itself.

USEFULNESS OF THE USELESS, UTILITY OF FUTILITY

The Taoist knows the Use of the Useless, the Utility of Futility, brings Spirit close to Life-Destiny, finds the Way Home, Truly Whole. This is to Embrace the One, to be Woman not Man, to Resonate with All-under-Heaven, to have an Inner Power that is Whole.

CLARITY AND CALM, MIRROR

The Taoist's Heart-and-Mind is a Bright Mirror. It reflects but does not absorb. It is Still Water. It is Tranquil, Calm without a ripple. To Attain Clarity
and Calm, to Purify the Human Heart-and-Mind, is to be truly Alive, it is to
Witness the Quickening of the Heart-and-Mind of the Tao, the Return of the
Real. The Taoist's Heart-and-Mind is the Tao, the Tao is the Taoist's Heart-
and-Mind, Still as Water, Bright and Clear as Radiant Sky and Lustrous
Moon, Outer Radiance containing Inner Marvel.

DARK LIGHT, INNER LIGHT

True Taoists care nothing for Fame. They hide their Light. They are incognito.
To Know Self, to wear sackcloth but to have jade in one's bosom, is to have
True Knowledge within. To follow the True Light of the Tao is to search in
the Dark.

RESONANCE, CONNECTION

When things or people Resonate, they also Connect. They are in tune with
the Cosmos, with Change, they are in Harmony with the Tao.

SILENT MUSIC OF THE TAO

The inaudible Song with neither Words nor Music—that is the Tao. Its Com-
pletion is slow. This is the Great Music of the Tao, too Faint to be heard. The
Tao itself is Silence. To Attain the Tao is to dwell in Non-Action, to live in
No-Business, to enter the Realm of Silence, which is the finest Music of all.

SOFT AND GENTLE

When men are born, they are Soft and Gentle, alive with Numinous Breath-Energy, Embracing Spirit within. The Taoist is Soft and Gentle as Water, is Beneath not Above, absorbs filth, accepts Misfortune and Calamity. Unexpected hardship, which Others find overwhelming, is overcome by the Taoist through the Soft and Gentle. This is the paradox, the Truth, that Soft and Gentle Prevail over Hard and Strong. The Practice of the Tao is Soft and Gentle, it leads to Endurance and Long Life.

RETURN, TURNING

The Tao moves like this, in Cycles. It Turns, it moves round, backwards, in reverse motion. It Returns to the Primal State of Simplicity, to the Root. It revolves, according to the constant Transformations of Change. The Taoist Turns away from the world, Returns to Self, to basic Nature. This is to Return Home, to the Uncarved Block, to the Inchoate Fog, to the Infant. This is to put aside the Human Heart-and-Mind, to Attain the Heart-and-Mind of the Tao.

RETREAT, RETIREMENT, SECLUSION

Through Retreat, by withdrawing into Inner Contemplation, the True Gentleman engages in Self-Cultivation and Achieves Inner Power. Small Men cannot come near him or cause him Harm. The Tao seeks no recompense. The Taoist, having Achieved, Retires to Seclusion and never dwells on Achievement. To withdraw into Retirement in the wake of Accomplishment and Success, to Let Go, averts Calamity. The Taoist follows the Cycle of the Tao, of Heaven-and-Nature, according to which the sun declines from its zenith, the moon waxes only to wane, flowers bloom only to fade, the greatest joy turns to sorrow.

ALSO AVAILABLE

THE STORY OF THE STONE, VOLUME I

The Golden Days, Chapters 1–26
Cao Xueqin
Translated with an Introduction by David Hawkes

THE STORY OF THE STONE, VOLUME II

The Crab-Flower Club, Chapters 27–53
Cao Xueqin
Translated with an Introduction by David Hawkes

THE STORY OF THE STONE, VOLUME III

The Warning Voice, Chapters 54–80
Cao Xueqin
Translated with a Preface by David Hawkes

THE STORY OF THE STONE, VOLUME IV

The Debt of Tears, Chapters 81–98
Cao Xueqin and Gao E
Translated with a Preface by John Minford

THE STORY OF THE STONE, VOLUME V

The Dreamer Wakes, Chapters 99–120
Cao Xueqin and Gao E
Translated with a Preface by John Minford

 PENGUIN CLASSICS

Ready to find your next great classic? Let us help. Visit prh.com/penguinclassic